MASTERING
Raspberry Pi 4
Projects

In 1 Hour

A Simple Guide to Program, Develop and Setup Unique Projects on

Raspberry Pi 4

COLIN
SCHMITT

Copyright

Contents

CHAPTER ONE

INTRODUCTION

The Raspberry pi refers to a collection of unitary-board made by the Raspberry foundation (a charity group situated in the United Kingdom, whose goal is to provide people with easier access to computing education, educate people and minimize digital divide.) Globally, users around the world learn programming with this device, carry out home automation, develop hardware projects, certain industrial applications, and lots more.

The Raspberry Pi has been presented as a miniaturized type of a computer whose size isn't much larger than a deck of cards. Its design is more like a system on a chip, which incorporates the CPU, and the GPU in a single integrated circuit, with the USB ports, Ethernet ports, RAM and parts attached into the board, for a complete package. Also, Raspberry pi series are very cheap and pocket friendly. The Raspberry pi computer is operated by a Linux operating system, and as well has a set of general-purpose input/output (GPIO) pins that grants you access to control electronic components for basic computing and research into the internet of things (IoT). The pioneer Pis were embedded with a 700MegaHertz CPU, and just 256MegaBytes of RAM, however, recent models are definitely improved versions due to the fact that they are embedded with quad core 1.4 Gigahertz CPU and 1Gigabyte of RAM.

The cost of most of these devices has always been attractive too as most models have always been priced at $35 or even less. So far, only four generations of the Raspberry

Pis have been created, they are Pi 1, Pi 2, Pi 3, and Pi 4, and each of these generations are designed to have a model A and a model B variant. Usually, the model A costs a bit less, and has reduced RAM size and ports (USB, Ethernet). Additionally, there's a Pi zero which is a subset of the Pi 1.

What is the Raspberry Pi 4?

The Raspberry Pi 4 is the most recent rendition of the Raspberry Pi computers; it was launched in June 2019. Being the latest model, one would definitely expect it to have some amazing features in terms of Raspberry Pi designs, which it does have. These features include a 1.5GHz quad-core ARM CPU, a 500MHz VideoCore VI GPU, and 1GB of RAM. There's a model with 4GB of RAM, however it has a higher price. The Raspberry Pi 4 Costs as little as $35, and $55 for the 4GB RAM version.

The Raspberry Pi 4 can carry out a great deal of work as beginner tech maniacs utilize the Pi board in various ways such as file servers, media centres, routers, network-level ad-blockers, out-of- date game consoles, and that's not all. There are numerous projects in the outside world in which people have used the Pi to develop various computing gadgets including phones, tablets, laptops, robots, smart mirrors which are keenly important in space exploration, and even other low-end products.

Without doubt, the Pi 4 is a more efficient model when compared to other Pi models as it can easily decide 4k videos, it also has an added advantage of quicker storage owing to the USB 3.0, and with a swift network accessibility through the embedded Gigabit Ethernet, it serves as a portal to countless new uses. Interestingly, the Raspberry Pi 4 is the first Pi that has a dual-screen feature, which means that it can support two screens simultaneously. It is also capable of supporting up to dual 4K at 30p displays; this is advantageous for users who desire additional desktop space.

Getting Started With the Raspberry Pi 4

It is paramount that you know that in the mundane form, the Pi is just a piece of square-board with various electronic devices soldered to it. Additionally, you'll need a monitor/TV, power supply, a micro HDMI cable to interface it with the monitor/TV, keyboard and a mouse. As soon as you link all the cables, the general method that beginners employ when setting up the Pi is to download the NOOBS(New-Out-Of-Box Software) installer. This installer permits you to install different operating systems, however, the official operating system, which is also recommendable for first time users, is the Raspbian Operating System. Here are the procedures you should follow to get the Pi 4 up and running:

- **Connect Your Raspberry Pi 4**

Attach everything that needs to be connected to your Raspberry Pi 4, ensure that these components are ported correctly and appropriately so as to ensure the safety of these components. Input the SD card into the micro SD card slot located on the opposite side of the Raspberry Pi 4 board. The SD card you intend to use must have been earlier set-up with Raspbian via NOOBS

Locate the USB connector end of your mouse cable and insert it to a suitable USB port on the Raspberry Pi 4, the port you input it doesn't matter, as long as it's suitable. In the same manner, connect the keyboard to the Raspberry Pi 4.

Ensure that you connect your output device (monitor/TV) to a power source and it is switched on. Observe the High-Definition Multimedia Interface (HDMI) port on the

Raspberry Pi 4 board, you'll notice that one end of the HDMI ports are uniformly flat. Now, utilize an HDMI cable to interface the screen (monitor/ TV) to the Raspberry Pi 4' s HDMI port. Connect your screen to the first HDMI port on the Raspberry Pi 4 board, this first port is tagged as HDMIO. Likewise, you can connect a second screen if you want to in the same manner. However, at this stage, nothing will be displayed to you on the screen, reason being that your Raspberry Pi 4 isn't active yet.

If you intend to provide your Raspberry Pi with an internet connection through Ethernet, connect an internet router or an Ethernet wall socket to the Raspberry Pi 4 with the aid of an Ethernet cable. In case you don't intend to connect to the internet or you prefer a wireless means of connectivity, the Ethernet cable connection is not necessary.

Although your screen (monitor/TV) has speakers that produce sounds of satisfying quality, you can still go ahead to connect headphones or speakers via the audio port on the Raspberry Pi 4 board.

- **Start Up Your Raspberry Pi 4**

Raspberry Pis are not built with a power switch, once they're connected to a power outlet/ source, they're turned on. Plug the USB power adapter to a power outlet and insert the other end of the cable into the Raspberry Pi 4's power port. A red LED light will be seen on the Raspberry Pi 4, this red light informs you that the Raspberry Pi 4 is connected to an active power outlet.

It then enters the booting stage. While booting, raspberries will be displayed at the crest-corner of your screen. You just need to hold on for a few minutes here and the Raspbian desktop will be displayed on your screen.

- **Complete the Setup**

When you operate the Raspberry Pi for the first time, there's a "Welcome to Raspberry Pi" application that assists you with the initial setup up process, it pops up automatically and guides you through the process.

When the "Welcome to Raspberry Pi" application comes up, click Next to initiate the start up.

Choose your language, country, time zone and go on to click Next.

Input your preferred password for your Raspberry Pi 4 , then click Next.

Select a Wi-Fi network to connect to and click Next.

At this point, the Raspbian checks for any recent updates to Raspbian and installs them, this takes a while.

After the installation process, click done or reboot the device to complete the update.

Guided Tour of the Raspberry Pi 4

The Raspberry Pi 4 was designed as an affordable machine that would aid children to learn and understand the working principles of the computer, but has clearly achieved more than it's fundamental aim. The Raspberry Pi can fill in as a replacement for desktop computer, particularly if you're using the 4GB version of the recent Raspberry Pi 4 model B, not forgetting other innumerable uses of this board such as virtual assistant, media center, file server, weather station, great performance clusters, game console, robotic control and lots more. The Raspberry Pi has served as the bedrock of some superb creations, and is even recognized by the International Space Station.

In terms of getting the Raspberry Pi up and running, it's a somewhat different task, and a bit complex, when compared to the average desktop computer, just slight variations. To make things easier, some online easy-to-follow guides and instructions, as well as the NOOBS (New Out-of-Box) software have been provided along with the device so as to facilitate quick and easy set- up of the device.

Contingent upon what you have in mind to do, NOOBS can install different operating systems, for instance, it can install the Raspbian OS for a desktop PC oriented purpose, or the software OSMC (Open Source Media Center) for media center oriented functions. However, Raspberry Pi's official Operating System is the Raspbian Operating System, and once it is installed, the entire basic functions are almost entirely the same with that of a desktop computer; you'll also be able to select applications from the recommended software menu. On the very first boot, the Raspbian OS directs users to a set-up wizard that initiates Wi-Fi connectivity and additional start-up tasks.

However, the price of the Raspberry Pi has been a discouraging factor for some people who are of the opinion that asides purchasing the single board for $35, setting-up a Raspberry Pi successfulness requires you to either purchase or own a keyboard, mouse, monitor/TV (Screen), power supply and an SD card. Summing up the cost of these devices gives you an amount that exceeds the price of the Raspberry Pi itself; however, the manufacturers are of the view that almost all households have all or some of these additional devices.

Due to recent improvements in the specifications of these Pi gadgets, coupled with the recent discoveries made about the usage of these Pi boards, people have invented new uses for the boards. Basically, the Pi runs a surfeit of Linux- based operating systems, in spite of that, the stable versions of Operating Systems it can run increases every time. Already, it runs the series from the esteemed RiscOS, and is also expected to be active on other operating systems such as the AndroidOS, chromiumOS etc. Furthermore, Pi is capable of running Windows without any hassle. The Raspberry Pi runs Windows 10 IoT core, an abridged form of the windows 10. The Windows 10 IoT core is not programmed to run a PC, rather it aids hardware hackers prototype Internet of Things (IoT) devices utilizing the Pi.

Also, as earlier stated, there are four generations of the Raspberry Pi, though Pi boards of any particular generation differ in model. Starting from the Raspberry Pi 1 which has the model B and the model A which has lesser specifications available, the Raspberry Pi 2 has only the model B available. However, the Raspberry Pi 3 is available as the model A, model B and model B+ variants, while the Raspberry Pi 4 only has the model B variant available. Generally, the model A variant has the is devoid of the Ethernet, has lesser memory relative to B, and possesses only a single USB port. Definitely, the model A variant costs less with a price of $25.

Arguably, the Raspberry Pi 4 model B is a more preferred choice than the Raspberry Pi 3, due to that fact that the Pi 4 provides you with better specifications at the same price. Moreover, the Pi 1 , being a less powerful model is cheaper than the Pi 3, and as well available in more portable, less power consuming model A rendition. A derivative of the Pi 1 is the midget Raspberry Pi zero that costs just $5. Regardless of the low price tag, the Pi zero can still carry out a significant amount of useful work. Based on the Pi zero's low price, petite size, as well as the low power consumption, it is crystal-clear that it has limitations compared to the bigger Pis. The Pi zero is provided with just one USB-otg port, and is not built with network connectivity. In contrast, the $10

Pi zero model supports the Bluetooth 4.0 feature and Wi-Fi connectivity. That being said, one would know that the Pi zero isn't much suitable to be used as a home desktop computer replacement but can still be utilized as a solitary IoT device or other automated uses that require minimal power usage.

CHAPTER TWO

Items Essential for Setting up the Raspberry Pi 4

As earlier stated, the raspberry pi doesn't work alone, it requires other peripherals to be attached to it. If these items are not present, the Raspberry pi will remain a piece of boards, which has metalloids soldered to it. These items are:

- **A Power Supply**

Earlier versions of the Raspberry Pi use a micro-USB for power delivery purposes. However, the Raspberry Pi 4, unlike its predecessors, uses a USB Type-C cable. Although some phone chargers might fit it in well and charge the Raspberry Pi 4 satisfactorily, it's advisable that you purchase a charger specially made for Pi 4, such as the power adapter provided by the Raspberry Pi foundation. The reason being that your standard phone chargers might not be consistent (in this sense, appropriate) to deliver sufficient power to run the board and its operations.

Moreover, another essential factor about the power supply to power the Raspberry Pi 4 is a good power supply that can generate at least 3A at 5V or 700mA at 5V for the Pi 4 model B. Other models may have different figures. Another vital factor to take note is that low-current, especially below 700mA, might cause the Pi 4 to reboot intermittently if it draws too much power, therefore it is strictly advisable that you don't use it for the Pi 4 as it's not suitable.

- **A micro SD card**

The SD card you plan to use for storage on the Raspberry Pi 4 should be at least 8GB class 4 or a class 10 micro SD card. The Raspberry Pi 4 uses this SD card to store programs, games, photos, files, and boots from it because the operating system is installed from the SD card. Getting a suitable microSD card for the Pi 4 is one issue, you'll also need a microSD card reader interface the card to a personal computer, Linux computer or Mac, the most feasible way to get this done is by using a micro SD card to SD card adaptor or a micro SD card to USB adaptor.

Albeit, the premier models of the Raspberry Pi use a regular SD card, the recent versions, including the Raspberry Pi 4, are designed to use a micro SD card for storage. However, not all microSD cards are compatible with Pi boards; hence the best option is to buy a Raspberry Pi microSD card. Asides from being perfectly compatible with the Raspberry Pi boards, the Raspberry Pi microSD card also has the added advantage of having the operating system already preloaded on it. Likewise, you can make use of the SanDisk 32GB ultra as it has been stated to be compatible.

- **Mouse, keyboard, and micro HDMI cable**

You don't have to connect the mouse and the keyboard to the Pi 4 board all the time, however, this depends on your project. Also, if retro gaming is part of what you'll be doing on the Pi 4, you might want to get a USB gamepad too. Moreover, you can purchase these items together in the official Pi 4 kit. Any standard USB mouse and keyboard will work perfectly with the Raspberry Pi 4. Likewise, wireless keyboard and mouse also work well when they're paired. Furthermore, any HDMI or DVI monitor/TV would work very well as a display for the Pi 4.

- **Computer**

Additionally, another essential item you'll need, at least for a start, is a computer. It could be a Windows computer, an Apple Mac computer, or a Linux computer. The purpose of a computer in the setup is to format the micro SD card when you connect it to the computer and download the initial setup programs for your Raspberry Pi 4. The operating system you'll download on this SD card is totally dependent on you and not the Computer, whose job is just to transfer files into your SD card.

- **Ethernet cable**

Otherwise known as the network cable, and as the name implies, the function of this cable is to connect your Pi 4 to a local network.

- **Audio Lead**

With this, audio can be played through headphones or speakers with the aid of the embedded standard 3.5mm audio jack. In the absence of an HDMI cable, an audio lead will be needed to produce sound. This implies that a separate audio lead isn't required if you're using the HDMI cable to connect to a monitor/ TV with speakers, because the audio can be played through the display.

- **A case**

To be candid, this is optional, but it is recommendable. Having your Pi 4 board encased provides it with more protection from direct mechanical and chemical damages gives it a more fancy look and makes it easier to use. Some of the cases, for example, the FLIRC case, have an inbuilt heat sink component, and this makes it a great option. Indeed, there are many types of such cases with fascinating designs such as transparent cases and retro gaming cases.

Setting up the Raspberry Pi 4 Operating System

As soon as you've got the necessary items, you're set to install an operating system on your Raspberry Pi 4, so you don't waste any more time not using it. The official and recommended operating system for the Raspberry Pi 4 is the Raspbian Operating System. As earlier stated, you can install different types of operating systems on your Raspberry Pi 4 depending on your purpose of use. To install the Raspbian Operating System on the micro SD card, a set of software called the New-Out-Of-Box Software (NOOBS) will be used, as this is the easiest and quickest way to get the Raspbian Operating System installed on the Pi 4. However, to entirely save yourself a bit of the stress and catalyze the step, purchase the NOOBS pre-installed 16gb micro SD card.

- **Download the SD card Formatting tool**

Firstly, download the SD card formatter from the SD card Association website on the computer. Then attach a microSD card to the computer (Windows, Linux, or Mac) and open the SD card formatter, click yes to allow your computer to run it. In case the SD card isn't recognized automatically after inserting it, remove it, reinsert and click "Refresh" on the screen. The computer should automatically select the card, but if it doesn't, you can select the SD card yourself from the list.

- **Format the SD card**

Select the Quick Format option and click format, input your admin password if required. When the formatting process has been completed, the card is deemed ready for use on your Raspberry Pi 4. Do not remove the SD card from the computer for now, and take note of the location of the formatted SD card as your computer will assign it to a hard drive letter (For a Windows computer), or it will be stored as a part of the finder window (on Mac)

- **Download NOOBS**

As earlier stated, the general method of bringing in the Raspbian Operating System to your Raspberry Pi 4 is by installing NOOBS (New-Out-Of-Box Software). Select "Download zip," contrarily, if you know how to install using torrents, you utilize the Torrent file instead of downloading zip. NOOBS provides you with a rundown of the operating systems and installs them for you. Then click Download zip and select the location of the file to be your download " folder." After the zip file has been downloaded, double-click the file to display it, and then uncompress the folder. A crucial thing you must do is that you have to copy all your files from the NOOBS folder to your SD card folder. To select all the files, press CTRL+A on your computer (⌘+A if you're using a Mac computer), then drag the entire files to the SD card folder that is displayed on your computer and wait for it to confirm that the files have been successfully copied. Now you eject the microSD card and detach it from your computer.

- **Insert the MicroSD card into the Raspberry Pi 4**

At this juncture, it is time to set up your Raspberry Pi 4 manually. Flip the Raspberry Pi 4 board over, and you'll see the microSD card slot underneath, insert the microSD card carefully. It fits in properly in only one way, so if the side of the microSD card you're trying to insert isn't yielding, turn the microSD card over and try inserting it again. After inserting the microSD card appropriately, start your Raspberry Pi. You must have connected the Pi 4 board to the peripherals earlier mentioned, in that manner, inspect your monitor to ensure that it is has a proper connection to the Raspberry Pi board, and that the HDMI cable is connected and fitted correctly into the HDMI ports of both the monitor and the Raspberry Pi 4. Also, check the keyboard and mouse, their cables, and connecting ports.

- **Power Up the Raspberry Pi 4**

The Pi 4 board isn't built with any button that switches it on or off, when you connect it to a power source, it will power on. When you plug in the Pi 4 board to a power outlet, hang on for a while, the boot up screen is displayed on your monitor. When the NOOBS installer is displayed, you'll be provided with a list of operating systems, the operating system we intend to use is the Raspbian Operating System, so you'll just proceed to install that. To obtain access to additional operating system options, click "Wi-Fi networks" and input your wireless passcode, a page that provides you with more operating system alternatives will then be displayed.

The installation process requires some amount of time, but it will definitely get completed, after which a message confirming the installation of the software will pop up. Then click Ok, your device will reboot and load the Raspbian software.

Welcome to Raspberry

After rebooting and loading for the first time, the Raspbian operating system takes you to a "Welcome Screen". Press **Next** when it comes up, this displays a screen where you will set your time zone, language, and login password. Then select Wi-Fi connection, this enables you to go online, input the WiFi's password, and connect to it. Since you now have an active internet connection, click Next, this permits the Raspbian software to check for any operating system update, if there's any, the

Raspbian software downloads the update and reboots so that the update becomes active.

Well done! You've successfully set up your Raspberry Pi 4, the next thing is to start using it for the purpose for which you bought it. Click the Raspberry Pi's icon displayed at the crest-corner of the monitor to access apps such as the web browser, media player, image viewer, calculator, file manager, text editor, programming IDEs, games, etc.

CHAPTER THREE

Using your Raspberry Pi 4

It has been on your mind for a while now, you've always thought of purchasing it, and now you're the owner of a Raspberry Pi 4 board! But what can you use it for, don't worry too much, I'll also help you with that. The functions that will be mentioned are mainly for the Raspberry Pi 4, nevertheless, most of these functions are also applicable on the Pi boards, the Raspberry Pi zero inclusive.

-You can use the Raspberry Pi 4 in place of a PC.

This is probably the simplest use of the Raspberry Pi 4. Asides the Pi 4 board itself, there's the microSD card, screen (monitor/ TV), USB mouse, USB keyboard, power supply, Wi-Fi, Ethernet ports. All these peripherals combined and set up with the Raspberry Pi 4 gives a replica of a desktop computer with little or no difference in terms of function and output. Also, after setting up the device and starting it, you'll find the chrome browser and Libreoffice because they have been pre-installed on it.

Printing with the Raspberry Pi 4

Perhaps you own an archaic printer that you really cherish and you love using it, however, it cannot be interfaced wirelessly, you're probably thinking of throwing it in the refuse bin, aren't you? But you really do not need to dispose of it, just connect your Raspberry Pi 4 to your home network and obtain a print server software probably by installing the Samba file sharing, followed by the Common Unix Printing System (CUPS). This CUPS provides your printer with drivers, including administration consoles.

After the setup, configure the Raspberry Pi 4 to ascertain that all computers available on your home network can access the printer. That's simply everything you have to do. As long as your printer has a USB cable port, or ports for adaptors, you're good to go.

You can even go further to include airPrint support to your Pi Print server. Even though this natively available printing feature requires a specific app on iOS devices, Android tablets and smartphones, most recently- made printers offer support for printing from mobile phones. With the Raspberry Pi 4, you equally extend this feature to old printers.

Set up a Retro Gaming device

This is among the most common uses of the Raspberry Pi devices. The Raspberry Pi 4 functions as a perfect retro gaming machine, it is very portable and powerful enough to be in a number of ways. When it comes to retro gaming, the two main available options are the Retro Pie and RecalBox, other options can be utilized too. The important thing to know is that whichever option you go with, you'll need a suitable controller that will be subjected to some initial configuration. Several platforms can be imitated, and reviving the popular 16-bit game consoles on the Raspberry Pi 4 is possible.

Kodi: The Raspberry Pi media center

In some instances, the main reason why users purchase the Raspberry Pi 4 is to use it as a Kodi media center. Kodi is available as disk images and it has several released designs. In some cases, it can simply be included in the retro gaming components.

Additional cautions are provided when you install Kodi, atimes, there may be attempts to stream pirated items due to the fact that not all add-ons are available. Therefore, it is advisable that you install from the official Kodi archives which has safe and legal add-ons.

Setting up a Minecraft game server

You probably thought it was restricted to the retro gaming aspect alone, common, it isn't! As you already know that the Raspbian operating system has a unique mode of the Minecraft game installed on it, because you'd have seen it when you start up your Raspberry Pi 4. However, what you're still ignorant about is the fact that the Raspberry Pi 4 can also function as a game server, and it does this excellently, enabling you to access and play the game anywhere on your home network.

In case you own more than one Raspberry Pi device, setting one aside for the solid purpose of being a dedicated server will give you a superb gaming experience especially if you have numerous Minecraft fans to play with. Moreover, asides Minecraft games, other multiplayer network games such as Civilization doom, Quake etc. can also be set up on the Raspberry Pi 4.

Controlling a robot with the Raspberry Pi 4

There are countless robot- controller Raspberry Pi programs; they're so much that you do not know which one to choose. You might just decide to go with the robotics package provided on your Raspberry Pi 4, which becomes effective as soon as the Pi device is powered on and it directs your robot. Moreover, you might just go with your own design, developed from several components you have. With the satisfactory processing power of the Raspberry Pi 4, it will perform this function without any hassle.

Using the Raspberry pi to develop a stop motion camera

With a Raspberry Pi 4 coupled with a dedicated camera module, you can make a stop motion video. With the aid of the python programming language on the Raspberry Pi 4, an appropriate stand/ hold, or a standard tripod stand, a well-illuminated environment, this will be achieved, although it requires a lot of time. Also, in order to achieve good results, you should practice it a few times beforehand. Additionally, you'll need a python script to capture each image and a breadboard to place a button on. You should also include a soundtrack.

When you add slight modifications by changing the programming script of this method can allow you to make a time-lapse video with the Raspberry Pi 4. This is done simply capturing a single frame with a timed delay.

Broadcast a Pirate FM Radio station With Raspberry Pi

In case you have a message you intend to share, or you wish to communicate with a particular community or group of people whose locations do not have internet connection, one of the most probable means you can reach out to these people is through a Radio. Interestingly, the Raspberry Pi 4 can broadcast on the Frequency Modulation (FM) band. However, broadcasting over FM without duly obtained license is ILLEGAL. The Raspberry Pi 4 can only broadcast over short range, this way; it kind of keeps you out of trouble. This function is particularly useful in the undeveloped areas of the world. All you need is a solution of compact battery, soldering tools and your soldering skills. Any audio you wish to broadcast will first be loaded on the embedded microSD card and played in a loop.

Creating a Twitter Bot with Raspberry Pi 4

You must have come across several ads, sponsored contents, messages on Twitter; much of these things is caused by bots. Bots are programs that are developed for the purpose of sending messages. Some are however useful because they're sometimes from websites you frequently visit, however, most are annoying. A large portion of these automated bots is targeted spam.

In spite of that, there are certain things you can do with a Twitter Bot. Instead of using your online presence to post those messages, you can utilize the python application on your Raspberry Pi 4. Then, if your Raspberry Pi 4 has a constant connection to the internet, you can create a Twitter Bot. The main steps to go about this is to first register a Twitter app via the Twitter website that provides you with the Twitter API and certain codes(Python or nodes.js), your bot is set. Then, select the contents to be tweeted.

Setting up a motion camera security system with Raspberry Pi 4

In case you have a gut feeling that someone is trespassing your property, or someone is trying to burgle your house or uncommon things are happening in your house and you want to see for yourself what's happening and how these things are happening? An item that will be of perfect help to you is a security camera, and the Raspberry Pi 4 can help you with this. With the camera module or the Raspberry Pi inserted, you can set up a motion camera security system; in fact, you can use a USB webcam for this purpose. However, you'll need a high storage size microSD card or USB storage device to store the footage from these devices.

The Raspberry Pi 4 incorporates a motion software programmed for UV capture, whose function is to take footage from your webcam, alongside other functions. When all these have been put in place, the system starts to record anytime it senses motion.

Setting up a home automation with Arduino on the Raspberry Pi 4

The Raspberry Pi makes a perfect brain and interface for a home computerization framework. Combined with an Arduino, and operating the Nodes.js application Heimcontrol, home computerization is made conceivable through several far off controlled radio-empowered mains connectors. Heimcontrol allows you to empower or debilitate any gadgets connected to the connectors, by means of the Raspberry Pi, with signals communicated by the Arduino. This method's ideal in case you're searching for a way to acclimate yourself with the nuts and bolts of home mechanization. In any case, imagine a scenario in which you need a framework that pretty much works immediately, with brilliant home computerization apparatuses, and so on. Maybe utilizing hardware that is now ready for action in your home. Coupling a Raspberry Pi with OpenHAB should work perfectly.

Set Up an AirPlay Receiver with Raspberry Pi 4

It isn't simply remote printing that the Raspberry Pi can deal with. AirPlay is likewise an alternative, empowering you to transform your Raspberry Pi into a smart speaker.

In case you decide to stream audio from your cell phone through a DIY speaker set up? Using the Pi Music Box committed disk picture for the Raspberry Pi, and interfacing the minicomputer to an appropriate speaker, you can likewise stream sound legitimately from the web. Google Music, Spotify, SoundCloud and numerous different services are accessible. Furthermore, the Pi Music Box utilizes Spotify Connect, DLNA/Open Home, BubbleUPnP, has USB sound help, and Raspberry Pi sound card compatibility.

Stream Live Video to YouTube with Raspberry Pi 4

Another approach to exploit a Raspberry Pi Camera Module is to live stream to YouTube. However, this works with a Raspberry Pi 3 or later. While a perfect USB camera can be employed, the best outcomes are enjoyed with the official gadget. To begin with, this venture, you'll need your own YouTube channel prepared to utilize, and the libav-tools bundle installed.

Learn Coding the Raspberry Pi 4

Initially, when the Raspberry Pi was launched in 2012, one of its key agenda was to get kids coding. In any case, it isn't simply kids who can figure out how to code on a Raspberry Pi. Adults can likewise exploit the platform's built-in coding Items.

Sound complex? Well it isn't. A few bits of software accessible in Raspbian are embedded to help basic programming, however the most significant is Scratch.

Intended to take into account all levels, Scratch is a block-based programming instrument that shuns the complexities of inputting lines of code. Rather, you just drag the commands into place. You will notice the effect of your programming codes in the code view and export the code as a program to run. Scratch is sufficiently straightforward to manipulate lights associated with the Pi's GPIO, and sufficiently complex to program basic games.

Interfacing PC games to the Raspberry Pi 4

Think the Raspberry Pi is restricted to retro computer game simulations alone? Reconsider! As a matter of fact, with a Raspberry Pi 2 or later you can replicate the streaming abilities of the Steam Link. This basically implies you can transfer computer games from your PC to your TV through a Raspberry Pi. Like the Steam Link, you'll have to ascertain that the Raspberry Pi or the PC (ideally both) are associated with your router by means of Ethernet. This is typically because the speed required for effective streaming isn't achievable with just a remote setup

In contrast to the Steam Link, you can, however, stream games that aren't accessible on Steam. Our preferred technique for streaming games to your Raspberry Pi is via a free tool called Parsec. It offers 60fps video streaming, ultra-low inactivity, and is accessible for Windows 10, macOS, and Linux.

Build a Smart Mirror with Raspberry Pi 4

Ever planned to find the most recent news, film trailers, pop recordings, and traffic and climate data while doing another thing? The appropriate way to do this is via smart mirror, a gadget controlled by a Raspberry Pi. Typically, it is a dual mirror with a unique display positioned behind the glass. Any sort of mirror can be utilized for a smart mirror function; you should employ one that satisfies your requirements.

And the list goes on and on, this just elucidates that the Raspberry Pi 4 has a wide variety of uses.

The Chromium Operating System on the Raspberry Pi 4

What is the chromiumOS?

Chromium OS is an open-source and easily accessible operating system developed for operating web applications and perusing the World Wide Web. It is the advancement form of Chrome OS, a Linux distribution made by Google. Like Chrome OS, Chromium OS depends on the Linux piece; however, its fundamental user interface is the Chromium web browser rather than the Google Chrome interface. Chromium likewise incorporates the Portage package supervisor, which was initially evolved for Gentoo Linux. Because Chromium OS and Chrome OS use a web program engine for the user interface, they are situated toward web applications rather than desktop applications or mobile applications. Google originally distributed the Chromium OS source code in late 2009.

While Google oversees and releases Chrome OS, the operating principle of the operating system depends on an open source project, which is the Chromium OS. This has been delivered on different gadgets and with the massive influence from FydeOS project can be installed on the Pi.

Note that few different variants of Chromium OS have been made available on the Raspberry Pi and they have currently been halted; there is every possibility that FydeOS may be halted in future. All things considered, you may decide to download and develop from the original source code, which is the chromium official website (www.chromium.org).

Reasons to Install the Chromium Operating System on your Raspberry Pi 4

Several operating systems are accessible for the Raspberry Pi. While the default choice is used by many, an abundance of Linux-only Raspbian alternatives. However, Chrome OS provides us with something different which is cloud computing. The moderately low specification of the Raspberry Pi makes it perfect for Chrome OS. An operating system that is designed to run the majority of its software as web applications, depending on the servers used for the processing. In the event that your Raspberry Pi is set up with an Ethernet or remote connection, you'll gain from this computing dynamic. This could even permit you to set up your Raspberry Pi as a beneficial yet minimal budget personal computer. Another cogent reason to install the Chrome OS on the Raspberry Pi 4 is that it is built with a straightforward user interface; it is relatively easy to use. Google has been committed, over the years, to refurbishing and refining the operating system. These transformation efforts have been felt in the official release and the open source Chromium OS.

Items necessary to install the chrome Operating System on the Raspberry Pi

- A Raspberry Pi board
- 8GB microSD card or more.
- A Fyde operating system.
- 7-ZIP
- Etcher

- Alongside a keyboard, mouse, HDMI cable and monitor

Prepare your SD card for the Chrome operating system

The downloaded IMG file format is compressed in XZ design, so you'll have to uncompress this with an appropriate tool. 7-Zip is your most ideal choice on Windows; XZ can be uncompressed locally on Linux systems. Then, the IMG record should be stored in the SD card. The least difficult alternative here is the incredible Etcher instrument, which will likewise format your SD card. Download, install and run Etcher, at that point, click Select image to peruse for the Chromium IMG file. Following this, affirm the microSD card is recognized by Etcher. If not, reinsert the media in your computer's SD card peruse and hold up until it appears.

Lastly, click Flash to compose the data. A couple of moments later, Chrome OS will be installed on the microSD card, prepared to boot.

Booting the Chrome Operating System on the Raspberry Pi 4

After securely expelling the microSD card from your computer it will be prepared to start up in your Raspberry Pi. The primary boot may require a long time to finish. You'll then be instructed to finish the set-up procedures. In the event that you've utilized a Chromebook or Android gadget, you'll notice this. It's fundamentally a case of entering your Google account subtleties.

When you've signed in, a blank desktop that needs to be configured will be displayed. The launcher is positioned at one corner of the screen and the notifications are on the opposite side. Everything should feel somehow recognizable. You will observe that Chrome OS on the Raspberry Pi doesn't exactly look like the variant seen on a

Chromebook. For instance, the Launcher symbol on the window is a hover, as opposed to a 3×3 framework. This is to a great extent aesthetic, nonetheless, and has no effect on the performance of the OS. Thinking about what your initial step ought to be? Right-click the work area and choose Set Wallpaper.

The File Manager on Raspberry Pi 4

To assist you with being more familiar with the device, the Raspberry Pi incorporates a document manager application called File Manager. To keep documents sorted out, they're regularly placed in folders. A folder may contain one or more files. You can access the File Manager icon on the right side of the internet browser icon in the taskbar. It has the look of a battered file organizer. When you click the icon of the file manager, it opens. The figures that follow after that show the document list that appears.

Understanding folders in File Manager

File Manager displays a list of folders at one side of the windows. To see the documents inside an organizer, click it. The records show up on the right side of the window. If you want to see the files inside a folder, click the little triangle close to the folder's name. At the point when the folder is open — thereby showing the files inside it — the triangle focuses on the right side. At the point when an envelope is shut, the triangle focuses on one folder's name.

The total rundown of files is known as the directory tree since it's somewhat similar to an upside-down tree. The tree works down from a root, which is the super-significant everything-begins here folder. If you allude to these figures, you will observe that the super important root folder incorporates a ton of different folders. They keep the files and folders that make your Pi work. You can likewise observe an envelope called pi at the head of the rundown. This is your home folder. Each client on a Pi has a home folder. Since you are at home most of the time, File Manager includes it in the directory tree so you can reach it rapidly without searching for it in the primary tree.

Navigating the File Manager

The directory tree provides each file in your Pi with its own address — which happens to be the only rundown of folders you have to navigate to locate the document. Addresses resemble this:

/home/pi/mystuff/and_so_on…

Document addresses are likewise referred to as Paths. Reaching an address is somewhat similar to strolling down a path with numerous turnings

To pinpoint a record at that address:

- Click the/home folder
- Click the/pi folder inside home.
- Continue opening folders to glimpse inside them until you reach your desired folder. As you keep on opening an ever-increasing number of folders, file Manager consistently informs you about your location in the folder, so It's difficult to get lost.

Here's a genuine model, which takes you to the pre-introduced applications in your Pi:

/usr/share/raspi-ui-supersedes/applications

Check whether you can keep on clicking till you locate the documents. You'll have to move down the tree to have access to all the folders in/usr/share, on the grounds that there's a great deal of stuff in there. The accompanying figure informs you about all the applications in File Manager. The envelope incorporates the applications in the desktop menu and so much more. You can double-click on any of these items to open it.

The Raspberry Pi 4 Configuration Tool

- **Opening the Raspberry Pi Configuration Tool.**

The Raspberry Pi Configuration tool, otherwise known as the Raspi configuration tool, provides you with the options of changing numerous settings on your Raspberry Pi device, especially if you are using the desktop version of Raspbian. Opening the Raspi configuration tool is not so complex, you just need to adhere to the steps that will be listed below.

- You can obtain access to the terminal directly from the Raspbian desktop or you SSH into the Raspberry Pi. SSH represents "Secure Shell", it is an efficient way to wirelessly control a device including the Raspberry Pi. With the SSH, you can interact with the Raspberry Pi controls in the absence of a keyboard, mouse, or screen linked to it. Unlike other methods of interfacing with your Raspberry Pi, the SSH is solely for file access and command line.

- Input this command: sudo raspi-config. This provides you with access to the Raspberry Pi Configuration tool, hence we move to the importance of each item.

Change User's Passcode

The Raspberry Pi's default login code is very easy to obtain via Google search. As a matter of fact, you can guess the login details; therefore, it's important that you change these details to prevent unauthorized users from logging into your Raspberry Pi. This tool can be used to set a new and it is advisable that you do so. To clarify you on this, the Raspberry Pi user's fault password is "Raspberry," if you leave it like that, even a novice will log in to your account because it's very simple to guess. Another thing is, you cannot change the password of other users with this tool, and you can only change yours.

- **Network Option**

This menu provides you with the options about the network capabilities of the Raspberry Pi. Some things it entails are:

• **Host name:** This option enables you to set the network name of the Raspberry Pi device. It is of more use if you own several Raspberry Pis, and you intend to differentiate among them.

• **WiFi:** You can even put the WiFi SSID and the passcode in place with the aid of this tool, this tool is actually very easy to use if you've tried setting up the WiFi manually through the command line and it seemed difficult.

• **Network Interface Names:** This option permits you to either activate or deactivate the network interface names that might look easily predictable. By default, the option has been deactivated, and you can activate it if the need arises.

- **Boot Options**

The next item in the Raspberry Pi Configuration tool is in charge of how your Pi will boot. The preset manner is that the Raspberry Pi will initially boot into the desktop, which however does not seem perfect for most users

• **Desktop/CLI:** This option permits you to choose whether your Raspberry Pi should boot to desktop or command line.

• **Hold on for the Network at boot:** Perhaps you want your Raspberry Pi to hold on until it gets a network connection during boot, and then activate this option.

• **Splash Screen:** Select whether your Raspberry Pi should display a graphical splash screen or just the default text boot screen. The advantage the later has is that it appears to be handier in situations whereby you want to detect errors or you just go to the error log.

- **Internationalization option**

In case the need to change certain settings arises, settings such as your region, time zone, or to update your keyboard display.

• **Change Time zone**

This option can be used to fix and update the time zone shown on your Raspberry Pi, and as such, you will be able to set the actual time zone of the place you are. Just adhere to the directives, and you are good to go.

• **Change Region**

This provides you with the options of changing your locale/region

• Change Keyboard display

To be candid, loading all the available keyboard displays requires a few minutes. After loading, you have the freedom of selecting any keyboard layout you like. However, be aware that the US keyboard layout differs from the layout of the UK keyboard.

• Update WiFi country

It is advisable that you update this too to ensure that it's the same country you're currently residing in. Several countries have different legal channels that can be used for WiFi.

- ### Interfacing options

This option enables you to activate and deactivate certain Interfacing functions present on the Raspberry Pi.

• Enable Camera

It is vital that you activate this if you want to use the Raspberry Pi camera module. Simply dive in here, press the option and activate it.

• SSH (Secured Shell)

The option comes into play when you decide to activate or deactivate the SSH entry to your Raspberry Pi. Activating this will grant you access to your Raspberry Pi from a remote location. However, if using the 'Secured Shell' isn't part of your agenda, it's better you keep it deactivated. At any point in time that you intend to use your Raspberry Pi on a general network, then ensure that you've changed the password from the raspberry default password.

• VNC

VNC is a unique program that is developed to allow one device to remotely control another device. With the aid of VNC, your Raspberry Pi has a vast array of uses, for instance, you can utilize it to view your Raspberry Pi's desktop without the need of attaching a monitor. VNC is preinstalled on later renditions of the Raspberry Pi, therefore if you decide to interface with the Raspberry Pi via RealVNC, ensure you activate this option.

• **SPI**

This option allows you to activate or deactivate SPI kernel module functions, which are required by piface on the Raspberry Pi. SPI represents Serial Peripheral Interface. It permits you to interface a four-wire Serial link so that sensors, memories, and peripherals are made available.

• **I2C**

Allows you to activate or deactivate the I2C kernel module, so you're able to interface I2C devices.

• **Serial**

With this option, you can activate or deactivate shell and kernel messages from the serial links.

• **1-Wire**

Enabling the 1-wire interface is important if you're planning to use something like the DS18B20 temperature sensor or other devices that make use of the 1-wire protocol.

• **Remote GPIO**

With this option, you will obtain remote access to the GPIO pins and should only be activated if it actually needs to be used.

• **Overclock**

When you overclock your Raspberry Pi, you harness more power out of it. By default, the Raspberry Pi overclock settings is deactivated, and the CPU is placed at 700 MHz

However, you can decide to overclock it up to 1000 MHz with the aid of this feature. These values will differ contingent upon the version of Raspberry Pi you have. You should also bear in mind that overclocking might lead to higher instability and mitigate the lifespan of your Pi. It is also deactivated on later versions of the Raspberry Pi, such as the Raspberry Pi 3.

• Advanced Options

These options look like the final lot of choices in the Raspberry Pi Configuration tool and they're relatively more complex. You don't have to manipulate these options unless what you're doing exceeds the basics of the Raspberry Pi.

• Expand File system

You can ignore this option if you've earlier installed the Raspbian operating system through New-Out-Of-Box Software (NOOBS), this is because NOOBS itself expands the file system for its users. However, if you brought in the Raspbian image directly into the Raspberry Pi through an image rather than NOOBS, then your access will be restricted to only the first 3GB of the SD Card.

 You can utilize this option to boost to full SD card capacity, not 3 GB alone. This expansion will enable you to put more stuff onto the SD card, however, you have to reboot after activating this option.

• Overscan

If it happens that your TV has a black border at the sides, then it's most likely due to the problem of Underscan. On the other hand, if the stuff happens to be flowing off the screen, the issue is Overscanning. If the issue you're battling with is Underscan, you should activate this overscan option, it will help in fixing the screen. This can be edited more in the config.txt to achieve this so that images are displayed correctly on your monitor/TV.

• Memory Split

The memory split option permits you to adjust the capacity of the memory that is made accessible to the Graphics Processing Unit. You may need to enlarge or reduce this depending on what you want to do with the Pi.

• Audio

The audio option allows you to compel sound out of either the 3.5mm jack or the HDMI port. Basically, this option has been set to auto, which implies that it will automatically determine which output to send sound through.

• Resolution

In case you're not satisfied with the default resolution, then you can change it with this option. As the Raspberry Pi becomes more powerful, there is a likelihood that more resolution choices would be available to pick, so it's certain you will need to check this option later.

• Pixel Doubling

The pixel doubling option replicates every pixel on the screen by doubling it, therefore making the entire item twice as large. This option is handy on high-resolution screens or large screen TVs. Furthermore, it is a useful option for people who have visual impairments.

• GL Driver

Simply enables you to activate or deactivate the experimental GL driver. It's best to deactivate this option unless you're certain that you'll need it.

- **Update**

This option, as its name implies, will update the Raspberry Pi Configuration tool and other software applications to the most recent version. This tool is constantly being updated, therefore it is crucial to keep it updated.

- **About Raspi Config**

This option elucidates more about the Raspberry Pi Configuration tool if you intend to know more information.

- **Removed Features**

In case you're looking for other features, you can stroll down to locate them

- **Add to Rastrack**

You will find this option useful if you want your Raspberry Pi to be added to the global map of Raspberry Pi users around the globe, that is when you will use this option to have your Pi added.

- **Finish up with the Raspi Config Tool**

Click Finish when you're satisfied with the changes you have made. You might be inquired as to whether you might want the Raspberry Pi to reboot, it is typically best to permit it to reboot so all the changes made can be applied. However, if you change the size of your SD Card during the configuration, you might experience a delay during the rebooting process.

CHAPTER FOUR

Introduction to Scratch Programming

Scratch is a visual programming application that permits users to create animations and games via a drag and drop framework. This application enables you to build your own computer games, animations and interactive stories with the aid of basic programming skills without the essential need of having to write code. Scratch is a superb way to get young people to start programming on the Raspberry Pi. Even though scratch was developed for people who are newbies to programming, nevertheless, even experts might still find it a bit difficult at certain points; let's talk about the concepts of Scratch.

Projects

Projects are those items or anything that are built with scratch; they include stories, arts, animations, games, pen etc. Projects in scratch are made with a scratch project editor, and these projects can be shared globally with the aid of the Scratch Community. In other words, a project is a developed coding in scratch.

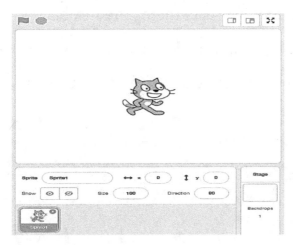

A scratch project

• Offline Editor vs Online Editor

Scratch provides its users with two varieties of editors. There's an online editor and an offline editor. Although these two editors look alike, there are slight differences between them. You can access the online editor clicking the "Create Tab" option on the website. The offline editor on the other hand, can be downloaded.

• The Interface

The users' Interface for the scratch programming application is divided into two aspects, which are: the project overseeing the environment and the project development. At the crest-corner of the Scratch screen, you'll find the Stage, it is displayed just above the image. Typically, the Stage is the platform in which scratch projects are carried out. Therefore, when one plays a game, the stage is the window in which it runs. As a default setting, the scratch cat is what you'll find in the Scratch Stage. This Scratch cat also happens to be among the numerous sprites or entities, buttons etc. in a scratch project. These entities or characters have been instructed to carry out what the Scratcher instructs them. The flexibility of Scratch enables the user to bring imaginative thoughts into reality and actually achieve the intended, and it is at this point that programming plays a role, as it enables the entities to carry out their functions.

• Programming

Prior to getting deep into the work-area, the most easy and useful way to perfectly comprehend how Sprites or entities are programmed in Scratch is by trying things out yourself. Here are some steps to put you through this task:

- Open the area displayed below in the Scratch program.

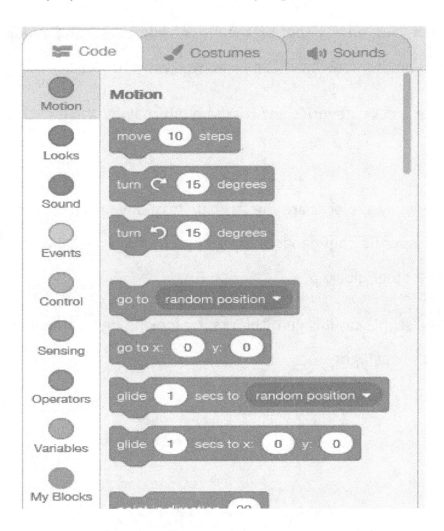

- Pick the blue "block" tagged move () steps and drag it towards the right portion of the screen.

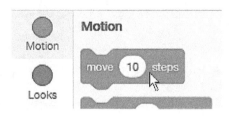

- Let go of the mouse so that you can position the block, ensure that the block is placed in the darker grey area, which is referred to as the Scripts area.

- After doing that, click on any spot on the block asides the white middle and observe the effects it has on the scratch cat, it moves by exactly 10 steps.

- Check the other block categories and try them out to know what each option does.

• **Blocks**

Just as its name implies, blocks are the basic units of any project on Scratch. They are embedded with specific commands that carry out unique tasks; a number of blocks can be put inside other blocks.

- Gather these "script" or linkage of blocks, by looking into various blocks based on their color and their category.

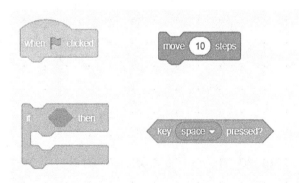

- Merge these blocks so they are in this manner:

40

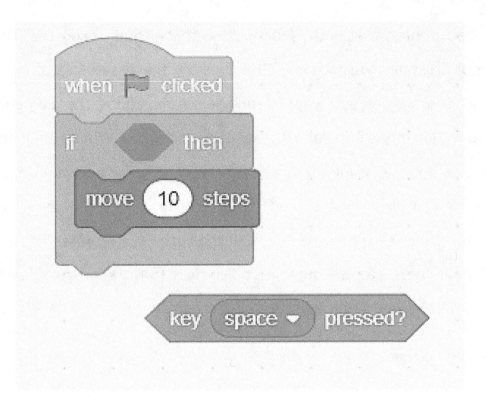

- Select the blue key sensing that seems to still be isolated and put it into the hexagonal input spot present on the orange "If" block.

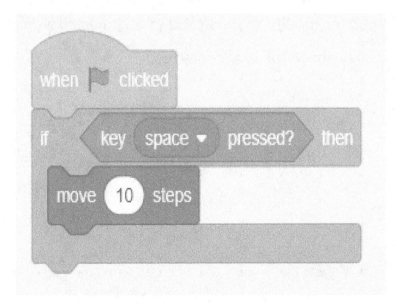

- Press the displayed Green Flag to put the project into action and observe its effects.

- You may be surprised that nothing happened, that's totally expected. The reason is you were not pressing the space key after pressing the Green Flag. If you don't hold down the space key when you want to run the scratch codes, there'll be no changes. Let me make that more detailed, the script starts with "When green flag clicked" which you have done. Clicking the Green Flag sets the script into motion starting with making the "When green flag clicked" block to run. When the script runs, it first notices "if the space key is pressed down," if the space key is pressed down, then the Sprite will move by 10 steps. Now that you're clear, run the program, and this time, hold the space key down and watch the Sprite move.

• **Paint/ Sound editors**

Scratch, of course, has a unique paint and sound editor. A paint editor can be said to be a program that is used to design and edit images. The paint editor in Scratch can be utilized to draw images for sprites. While the sound editor is a program that can be used to record, import or modify sounds used in a project. To display these editors, click on the tabs directly above the block palettes.

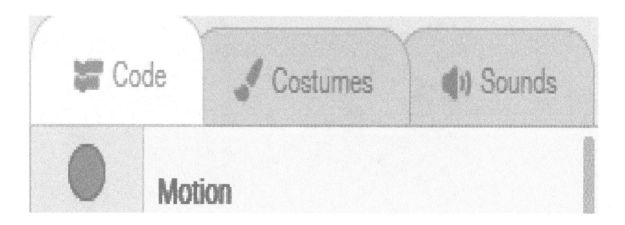

• Sprites

Sprites are best described as the characters of a particular Scratch project. Each Sprite has its unique blocks and they can interact with one another using Broadcasts. Also, each Sprite is capable of carrying out its functions, for instance, in a game whereby a dog is supposed to chase the Scratch cat, the dog has been instructed to chase the cat while the Scratch cat is being directed by the player. You'll observe that these two sprites have been programmed to carry different functions, in the same way, a program can contain over 50 sprites, each carrying out its function.

• Sprite Pane

Gaining access to different sprites can be done via the sprites panes, which are situated beneath the stage. A blue box will surround the sprite that you've currently selected. When you click any sprite, its details will be displayed.

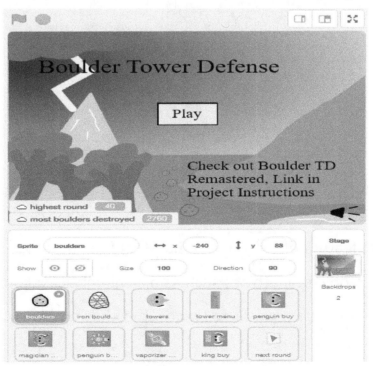

• Creating New Sprites

Nearly all the projects on the Scratch application require two or more sprites. At the bottom-corner of the sprite panes, there is a button that enables you to create new sprites. Pressing this button provides you with some options. You can bring in a new sprite with this option, either in the form of an image or as an entity, which initially has a script. The buttons go thus according to the image;

- Picking a sprite from the sprite library.

- Opening the paint editor to draw a sprite.

- Getting a random sprite.

- Bringing in an image from the computer via Scratch.

• Backdrops

Another important feature of a work is its background; backdrops are not motile but can be employed to do certain things such as playing music, sending a broadcast and other functions. In a similar manner to sprites, they have pictures that can be edited as well with the aid of a paint editor. Beneath the backdrops, there's a button whose function is to bring in a new backdrop.

• **Project Sharing**

This provides you with more options on how you can share projects.

Introducing Scratch User Interface 2.0

The Scratch User Interface can be said to be the environment of the Scratch program, which separates the screen into multiple panes. It follows this fashion: on the left side, you have the stage and the sprite list, in the middle, there are the block palettes, and situated on the right are the scripts, sound editors and costumes. The block palettes bear code units called "Blocks" imported to the scripts area so as to build projects. To prevent the block palette from being too large, it is sorted into ten groups of blocks, which are Motion, Looks, Sound, Pen, Data, Events, Control, Sensing, Operators, and More Blocks (custom-built blocks and extensions). The LEGO WeDo blocks and the PicoBoard blocks can be found in the More Blocks option.

• **Intent**

In the course of designing Scratch, the Scratch developers' utmost motive was to ensure that its language and environment were Intuitive, and could be easily understood by children who had no initial knowledge about programming. There is an absolute difference between highly effective general-purpose functions and multi-linked programming methods and the supposed limited array of the Scratch programming language. Therefore, tasks that can be easily done in high-level programming language are sometimes hard in Scratch, and vice versa.

• Palettes and Panes

The Scratch 2.0 user interface is simple and relatively easy to use. Its design enables users of all kinds and levels of experience to develop projects. As regards doing this, the program separates the different sections of the Scratch into Palettes and Panes

• Block Palette

The block palette grants you the access to drag blocks into the scripts area, develop variables, and create additional blocks. The moment you pull a block from the Block Palette, a duplicate of it goes with the mouse until the moment you drop it off at the spot where it is needed. The Block Palette has ten segments embedded in it.

• Script Area

You can bring in blocks originating from the block pallet into the scripts area by dragging them. These blocks are merged with more blocks to create scripts, and they eventually develop a project.

• Sprites Pane

The sprites pane entails a thumbnail view of the entire sprites.

- It entails the names of the sprites bearing a thumbnail of the sprites present costume near it.

- If you're active on the Sprites Pane, the thumbnail will change gradually to avoid annoyance. Nevertheless, if it's opened into the sprites information pane, it will transform at the present rate.

- You can include a new sprite by selecting any of these:

- **Giga:** This launches the window with Scratch Default Sprites.

- **Paint Brush:** Opens the paint editor. A new sprite will originate from what you paint.

- **Folder:** This opens the file browser, therefore enabling you to open a sprite or image file.

- **Camera:** Launches the camera and snaps a picture when you instruct it to.

- When you click on a sprite, it opens up either the Script Area or the Costume Pane.

- If you want to bring in a costume, you drag it to a different sprite and the costume will be inserted into that sprite's Costume Pane.

- Moving audio to a different sprite will duplicate the sound into that sprite's Sounds Pane.

- Moving a sprite onto another sprite will switch their positions in the sprite pane.

- Right Clicking a sprite provides you with a rundown containing four options:

- **Duplicate:** Produces a similar version of a sprite including costumes, scripts and sounds.

- **Delete:** Erases the sprite.

- **Save to local file:** Opens up a file browser that enables you to save your sprite together with any script in the selected sprite.

- **Show:** Displays the object in case it's concealed and sends it to the front.

- Moving a script from the thumbnail of one Sprite to the thumbnail image of another will copy the scripts to that sprite.

• **Sprites Info Pane**

The sprites info pane contains information regarding the sprites that have been selected and some tools for making adjustments on the Sprites. This pane is displayed when you click the blue (i) in the Sprites Pane.

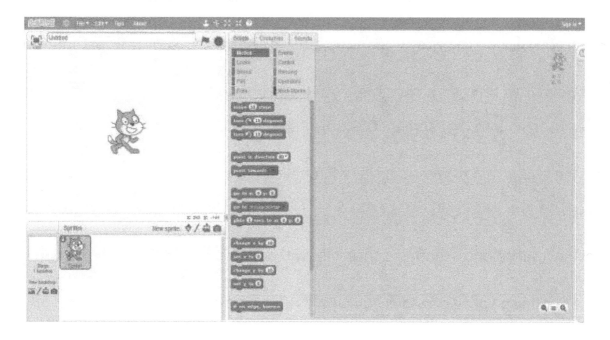

- You can change a sprite's name by clicking the box that has the sprite's name in it.

- Some adjustments can be made to the sprite's name by pressing any of these buttons:

- **Can Drag In Player:** Selecting this option will make the sprite draggable outside the editor.

- **Circular Arrow** — This permits full rotation of a sprite.

- **Linear Arrow** — Allows the sprite to face the left or right direction.

- **A large dot:** This disables the rotating feature of the sprite; it will keep on facing 90 degrees no regardless.

- Pressing and moving the blue line positioned over the sprite will cause the sprite to rotate.

- Double-clicking the sprite will return its orientation to 90 degrees.

- The sprite's X and Y coordinates and the directions are stated.

• **Costume Pane**

The costume pane bears the list of costumes of the sprites that have been selected

- It entails the name of the sprite as well as a preview image.

- When you click on a frame, the sprite transforms into that costume

- You can include new costumes via any of these options:

- **Giga:** This opens the scratch's embedded library on sprite and enables you to choose any costume.

- **Paint:** Brings in the paint editor

- **Import:** This opens the file browser, thereby permitting you to open a sprite file.

- **Camera:** This launches the webcam or external device to take a picture that will be used for a new costume.

- Adjustments can be made to costumes in the paint editor positioned at the right side of the screen

- You can rename a costume by clicking the box that bears the costume name.

- When you right-click on a costume, it provides you with a rundown of three options, these are:

- **Duplicate:** This makes a replica of the costume.

- **Delete:** This option erases the costume

- **Save to local file:** Saves the costume to whichever location you choose.

- You can rearrange costumes by moving them into the correct email order on the list.

• **Sounds Pane**

This pane entails a list of audio clips.

- The sound pane contains the title of the sounds, and the thumbnail of a speaker

- The sound will be played when you click the speaker icon.

- You may include a new sound to the list when you press any of these options:

- **Record:** This opens the sound recorder, and by so doing, you can record audio from an external device.

- **Import:** This opens the file browser, thereby enabling you to bring in an audio file.

- A sound can be played by clicking on the play button positioned near the speaker icon.

- A sound that is currently being played can be put to a halt when you press the stop icon, which is also located near the speaker icon.

- You can remove a sound by clicking the "X" button

- You can rename the sound by clicking the box that has the name listed in it.

- When you right-click a sound icon, it provides you with the following options:

- **Duplicate:** This makes a replica of the costume.

- **Delete:** This option erases the costume

- **Save to local file:** Saves the costume to whichever location you choose.

• **Stage**

The stage can be said to be a sprite that functions as the background of the project. Due to these functions, it has traits that are unique relative to other sprites. No sprite is enabled to move behind the stage, the stage will always be found at the background and likewise, it cannot move itself. There are two buttons you can find here, they are:

- **Green Flag:** This interacts with the "When Green Flag Clicked" block

- **Stop:** This halts the entire scripts in all sprites.

- You can move sprites to the stage by dragging them.

- The entire actions take place in the stage

• **Toolbar**

You will find the toolbar at the topmost section of the program, and it performs numerous functions in scratch. On the crest corner, you'll see the text "Scratch." Next to this text, you'll see the picture of a grey sphere, if you press this image, it provides you with a rundown of all the languages available in Scratch. Following this grey image, you'll find several options here.

- **File menu:** when you click this, it also provides you with various options

> **New** - This creates a new project from an empty template.

>**Save now** - This option saves the present project in the directory from the directory that it originated from. In case the file is new, it opens a file browser, which helps you to save the project as a new file, excluding when you're online.

>**Save as copy** - This creates a duplicate of the present project.

>**Go to My Stuff** — This button directs users to their My Stuff page.

>**Upload from your computer** — Opens a file browser, and by so doing, it opens a project. Opening this project this way prevents the sprites from appearing in the program you were previously working on.

>**Download to your computer** — This opens a file browser, inquiring the intended location for a current project to be saved.

>**Revert** — Transforms the project to the state it was during a previous save.

- Edit Menu

> **Undelete:** This reverses a recent delete command on a sprite, costume, sound, or script.

>**Small Stage layout:** Reduces the size of the stage

>**Turbo mode:** This sets the player into turbo mode. In turbo mode, codes are executed quickly.

- Tools

>**Duplicate:** This button, which is indicated by a stamp icon, makes a replica of anything that is displayed. It makes a duplicate of sprites, costumes, costume selections, sounds, blocks, and scripts

>**Delete:** The delete button is indicated by a scissors icon and its function is to delete anything that's on the screen. The delete button deletes sprites, costumes, costume selections, sounds, blocks, and scripts. There are also other options such as enlarge and shrink, which function when you click on a sprite in the stage, costume editor, or any selection at all in the costume editor will make the sprite or selection grow bigger or become smaller respectively.

CHAPTER FIVE

Project 1: Astronaut Reaction Timer

• **Introduction**

In this first project, your aim will be to make use of Scratch to develop a game that will test how fast your reaction is and analyze the distance travelled by International Space Station in the duration it takes you to react. Press the Green Flag to begin the game. Press the spacebar on your keyboard when you head the word "Go!"

• **Get Started**

Launch the Scratch Starter Project. For the online mode, open the starter project by clicking on this link: rpf.io/astronaut-reaction-timeson. If you prefer the offline mode, download the starter project and open it in the Scratch offline editor. If you prefer the offline version instead, download it from this web link: rpf.io/scratchoff. When you launch the starter project, a space backdrop and a sprite astronaut are what will be displayed, just like it is in the image below.

Things happen rapidly when you're travelling at 7.66 kilometres per seconds, and there has to be a quick reaction time when there's an encounter with a space debris to avoid collision. Furthermore, astronauts require a quick reaction time and steady hands so that they can easily carry out tasks such as controlling robotic arms. Astronauts are trained to have a speedy reaction to situations and to prepare them for every possible happenings.

Scientists at NASA have carried out several experiments to test the reaction times of astronauts. These tests were first performed on the ground, while they were on board and when they returned to the Earth. These experiments made them discover that astronauts took more than twice as long to react when they were in space. Therefore, the scientists made the propositions that this could have been due to stress and the brain trying to adapt to microgravity in space. They also stated that the reaction time of astronauts went back to normal after returning to Earth. Create a game in Scratch to examine your reaction skills, and ascertain whether you can do what Neil Armstrong did.

• **Begin the game**

Create the game in such a way that the astronaut provides the player with an introduction and basic guidelines at the start of the game. Then, press the astronaut sprite, then move a "When Flag Clicked" block by dragging and dropping it, then input "Say Hello! For 2 seconds" block.

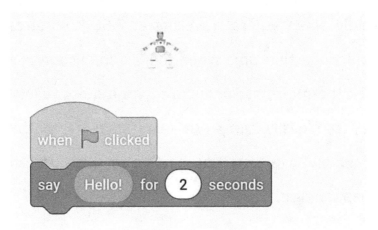

The next task is to convert the "Hello!" command to a different greeting. You can employ this write up below or come up with anything that suits you.

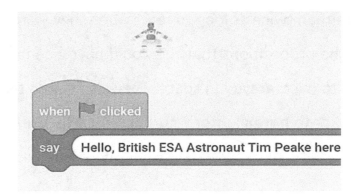

Afterwards, include a "wait 1 seconds" block and input some codes that will inform the players what to do next, whether they need to keep on waiting while it loads, or they should press any key or a particular key on the keyboard.

Now, press the Green Flag to test your game and ascertain whether it works.

• Include a random pause command

The game should start just immediately, and the beginning should be one that cannot be predicted by the players. Include a couple of blocks into your program to ensure it holds on for some seconds before it starts to run, and then make the sprite say " Go!". The blocks you'll include to perform this might be hints about how to make certain movements or techniques in the game.

• Calculate Reaction times

To work out the reaction time of the player, you can use Scratch's programmed timer. Include a "Reset Timer" block to your script.

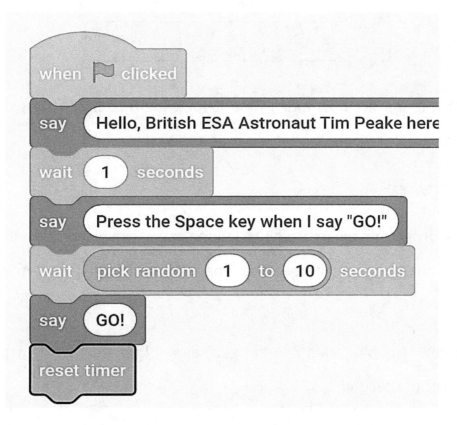

The timer will then start to count from zero seconds. The timer has to halt when the player presses the spacebar. Input the "Wait Until" block and a "key spaced pressed?" block to initiate the next aspect of the program.

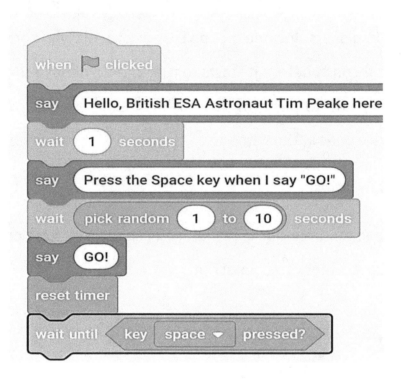

Then, inform the players how much time it took them to press the spacebar. Utilize "Join" blocks to state the number of seconds it took them.

● **Analyze Distances**

Now that the program is aware of the reaction time of the player, develop some codes to determine the distance International Space Station would have travelled in that duration.

- Bring in a new variable called Kilometres. Bearing in mind that ISS travels at about 7.66 kilometres per second

- Include blocks to your code so that the variable you've Just added (Kilometres) is tagged with the distance ISS would have covered.

• **Finish the game**

Here, the astronaut sprite has to inform the players of the distance they would have travelled on the ISS. To ensure your calculations are much easier to read, you can utilize a "Round" block. This will round up and approximate the number to become a whole number. Input it by using "Say", "Join", and "Join" blocks to inform the players of the values of "Kilometres" Variable.

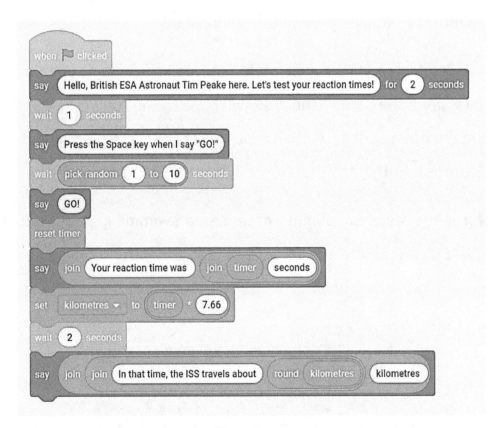

Well done! Now you can move on, try out other projects of your choice, and see what the outcomes are.

CHAPTER SIX

Project 2: Synchronised Swimming

• **Introduction**

This project will give you knowledge about how to program a synchronized swimming routine for Scratch cat with the aid of loops and creating replicas.

• **Swimming left and right**

In this project, a team of swimmers will be programmed to perform a rhythmical style of moves to a music. First, let's get one cat swimming.

Launch a new Scratch project. If you prefer the online version, open a new online Scratch project. If, on the other hand, you will go with the offline mode, then open a new project in the offline editor. Perhaps you prefer the Scratch offline editor, click on this link: rpf.io/scratchoff.

Now, transform the stage so that it resembles a swimming pool. You do this by clicking on the "Stage", then select "Backdrops" tab and press "Convert to Bitmap"

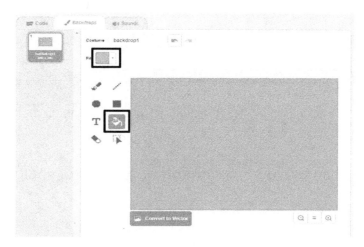

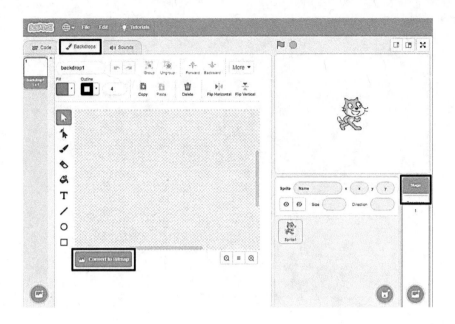

Choose a blue color and the "Fill with color" tool, after doing that, click the backdrop.

You have to use another cat sprite, therefore press the cancel button on shown on the walking cat to delete it.

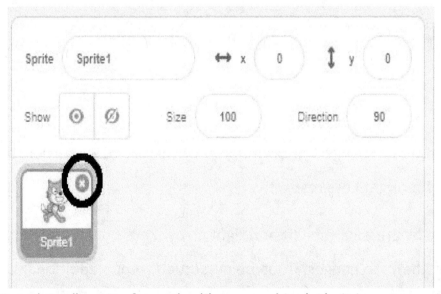

Select the "Cat Flying" sprite from the library and include it in your project. If you look at the Cat Flying from another view, it looks like it's swimming in space.

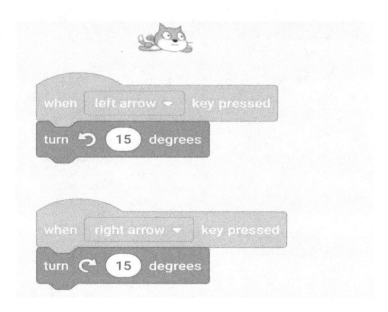

Now, let's get the cat swimming. Click on the "Cat Flying" sprite, then press "Code"

Cat Flying

and input this code to change the orientation of the cat to either left or right when you press the left or right keys respectively.

Verify your code by pressing the left and right arrow keys on your keyboard and see if the position of the cat changes. That being settled, input additional codes for the forward and backward movement of the cat.

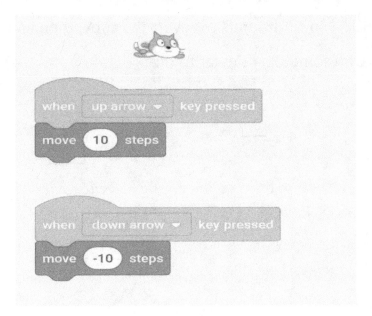

Now, put your codes into action by swimming around the stage utilizing the arrow keys.

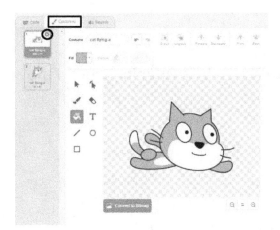

•**Costume**

You can as well change the costume of the Flying cat to any one you desire. Simply click on "Costumes" and erase the "Cat Flying-a" costume. Change the name of the other costumes from "Cat Flying-b" to "Right". After that, you right click on the costume and press "Duplicate" so that it creates a replica.

At this juncture, click" Flip Horizontal" to revert the copy, then you name it " left" and you should be left with something similar to this:

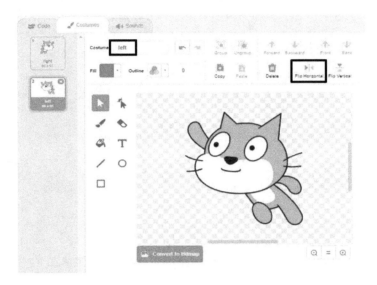

Press "Code" to revert your code and include blocks to alter the costume whenever the direction is changed.

Once again, put your codes into action by swimming around the stage using the arrow keys on your keyboard.

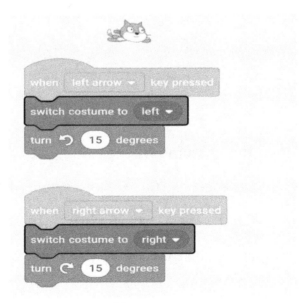

• Set Up the team

Synchronized swimming requires more than a cat, hence we'll use "Create Clone Of" to create replicas of the same behavior. To start with, include codes that will ensure that the cat always starts in the same orientation when you press the Green Flag.

Check if your code is active by pressing some arrow keys and then clicking the green flag to return to the start position.

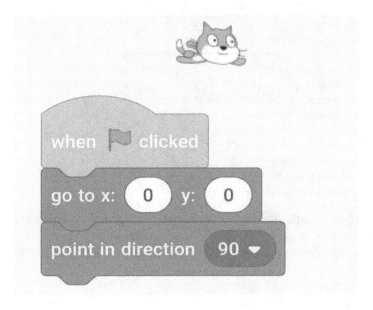

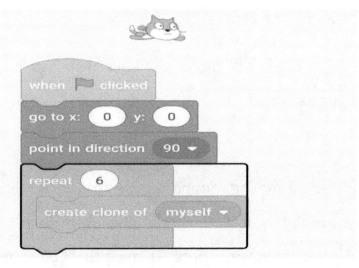

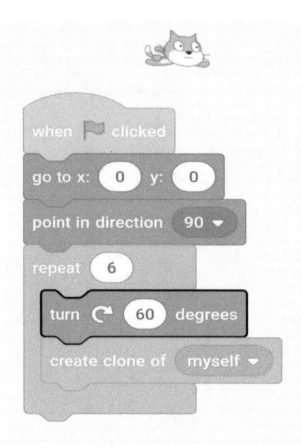

Now, we can employ a "Repeat" loop to create six replicas (clones) of the cat. Loops are used to do the same thing or generate the same results multiple times.

It's likely you would prefer the cats to be in different positions, input codes to rotate 60 degrees before creating each replica.

Check if your codes are active via the arrow keys. You can create some amazing synchronized swimming patterns!

• **Music**

This form of coordinated swimming routine requires music. Nevertheless, if you can't play sounds, you're absolutely free to ignore this step. Select a sound from the "Loops" section and include it in your sprite. Then go to "Code" and include the block to play your music. Also, including the "Play sound" inside a "Forever" loop implies that the music will keep on repeating.

Now you can run your project, to stop the music while it's playing, press the red button. If you want a routine that you can be perfect at and easily repeat, then you should include some moves to be performed when you press the space key.

Then run to programs and press the space key to check this new routine, but try moving to different positions using them arrow keys before you press the space key.

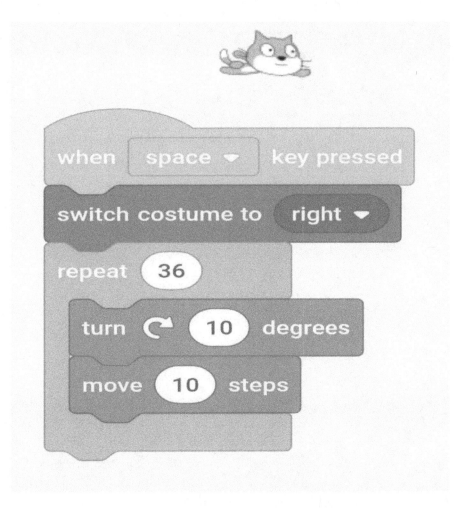

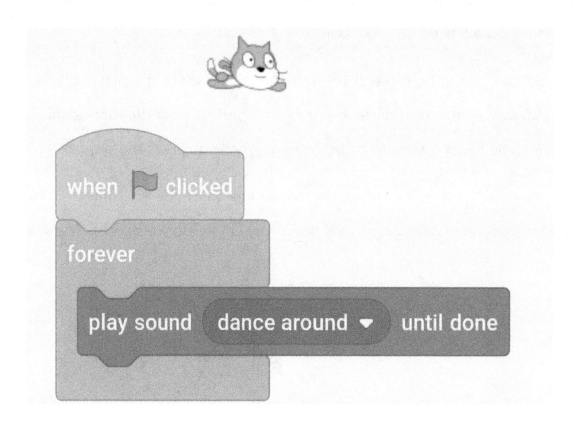

CHAPTER SEVEN

Project 3: Archery Game

• Introduction

This chapter will teach you how to develop an archery game, in which you have to shoot arrows as near to bullseye as you can.

• Aiming Arrows

Firstly, let's craft out arrows that move around the screen.

Launch the Scratch project. Like other games, if you prefer the online version, then open the Scratch starter project at rpf.io/archeryon. If you happen to have registered a Scratch account already, you can create a duplicate by clicking "Remix". On the other hand, if you prefer the offline version, simply open the Scratch starter project in the offline editor. If you prefer the offline editor, you can download it from this link, rpf.io/scratchoff. When you open the starter project, a target backdrop and a crosshair sprite will be displayed.

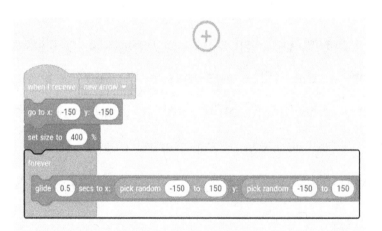

At the moment your game starts, broadcast a new message to shoot a new arrow.

After this message has been received and actualized, go forward to set the arrow's position and dimension. Now, press the Green Flag to run your game. You would observe that your arrow gets bigger in size and it moves towards the lower edge.

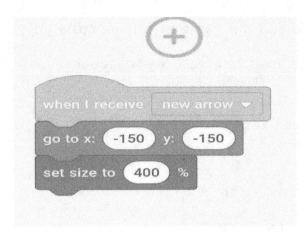

Input codes to your arrow so that it can "glide" randomly around the stage "forever"

At this point, test the game again, you should observe your arrow move randomly around the stage.

• Shooting Arrows

What you're required to do here is to instruct your arrow to shoot when you press the spacebar on your keyboard.

Put a halt to the other script, which is the script directing the arrow, whenever you press the spacebar.

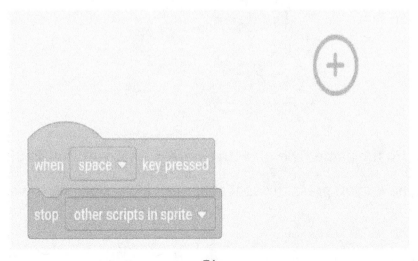

It is important that you run the game at this juncture so you can be sure that the arrow stops moving whenever you press the spacebar.

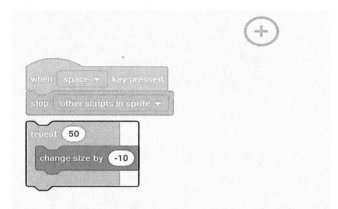

Now, the next thing to do is to animate your arrow to make it resemble an object moving towards its target.

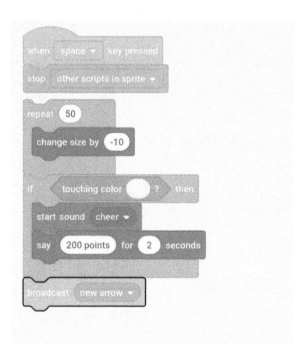

After that, test run the game. The objective here is that you should observe the arrow get smaller whenever you press the spacebar, as if it's propelling towards its target.

As soon as the arrow reaches the target, you can inform the players about the amount of points they've scored. For instance, if a player scores 200 points for hitting the yellow spot on the target. You can even go further to include a code that produces a sound whenever the arrows hits the yellow spot.

To end it all, you need to broadcast the "new arrow" message again to obtain a new arrow. Well done! Now, enjoy your game.

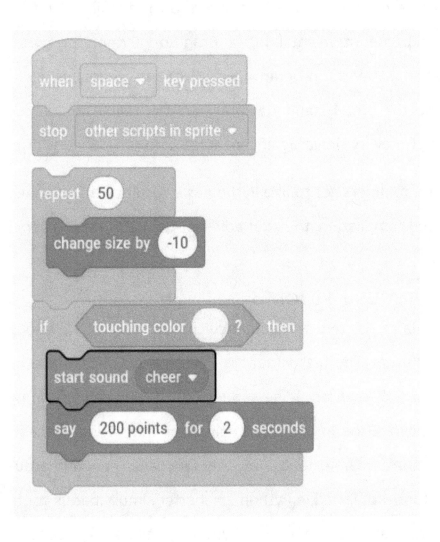

CHAPTER EIGHT

Using Python Programming Language on Raspberry Pi 4

Python is a deciphered, object-oriented, high level programming language with flexible semantics. Its elevated level underlying data structures, coupled with dynamic composing make it appealing for quick application development, just as its usefulness as a scripting language to associate existing parts together. Python's easy, simple to learn sentence structure hammers on readability, and by implication, it reduces the expense of maintaining a program. Python promotes modules and packages, which supports program seclusion and reuse of codes. The Python interpreter and the broad standard library are accessible in source or binary form without charge for every single significant stage, and can be freely dispersed.

Frequently, programmers get to like Python as a result of the efficiency it gives. Since users don't need compilation, the alter edit-test-debug process is very swift.

Python 2 versus Python 3

Python is available in two variants, which are distinctive enough to entangle numerous new users. The first variant is Python 2.x, which is the more established "legacy" branch, will keep on being supported (that is, get official updates) through 2020, and it may still be in use informally after that. Then there's Python 3.x, the current and future manifestation of the language has numerous valuable and significant features not found in Python 2.x, better simultaneous controls, and a more proficient interpreter. The adoption of Python 3 was eased back for a very long time by the general absence of third-party library support. Numerous Python libraries supported just Python 2, making it hard to switch. However, throughout the most recent few years, the amount of libraries supporting just Python 2 has dwindled; the entirety of the most well known libraries are presently compatible with both Python 2 and Python 3. Today, Python 3 is the most ideal choice for recent projects, there is no reason to go with Python 2, except you are left with no other options. Nevertheless, in case you are left with Python 2, you have different strategies available to you.

Introducing Thonny Python IDE

Thonny is a free Python Integrated Development Environment (IDE) that was particularly designed in view of the starting Pythonista. In particular, it has a worked-in debugger that can assist you when you run into terrible bugs, and it offers the capacity to do step through expression assessment, among other extremely impressive highlights.

Web Download

The web download can be gotten to through an internet browser by visiting the Thonny site. Once on the page, a dim light box will be displayed at the upper right corner. When you've seen the dim box, click the suitable link for your Operating System.

Command Line Download

You can likewise install Thonny by means of your system's command line. On Windows, this can be done by initiating a program called Command Prompt, if you happen to be on macOS and Linux; you initiate a program called Terminal. When you've done that, input this command: pip.introduce.thonny

The User Interface

To comprehend what Thonny really is, we need to know what it can do. Consider Thonny the workroom wherein you will make astonishing Python projects. Your workroom contains a tool stash containing numerous tools that will empower you to be a competent Pythonista. In this segment, you'll find out about each features of user interface that will assist you with utilizing each of your tools in your Thonny toolbox

The Code Editor and Shell

Now that you have installed the Thonny application, launch the application. A window with numerous icons will be displayed over the top and two white areas.

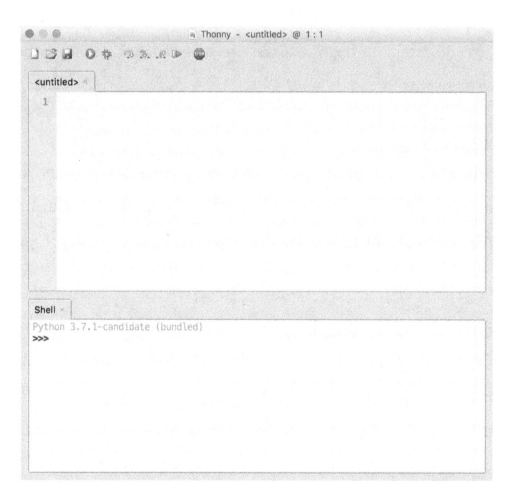

Notice the two fundamental areas of the window. The top area is your code editor, where you will input the entirety of your code. The base half is your Shell, where the outcome of your codes will be displayed.

The Icons

Over the top, you'll see a number of icons. You'll see a picture of the symbols beneath, with a letter over every one. These letters will stand in for each of these icons.

The Icons across the Top of Thonny's UI

A: The paper symbol permits you to create a new file. Commonly in Python, you have to put your programs into separate files. You'll often use this icon whenever there is a need to write codes and create programs in Thonny.

B: This icon represents an open folder. It grants you access to a document that, as of now, exists on your computer. This may be helpful on the off chance that you intend to return to a program that you have worked on previously.

C: The floppy plate icon, it enables you to save your code. You should remember to press this early and regularly. This will be useful every time you're writing a program in Thonny.

D: The play symbol enables you to run your codes. Recall that the code you compose is intended to be executed. Running your code implies you're telling Python, "Do what

I instructed you to do!" (In other words, "Read through my code and execute what I have inputted.")

E: The bug symbol enables you to troubleshoot your code, in other words, to debug your codes. This simply means you're checking for errors in the program, either line error, by inputting the line of codes in the wrong order or word error, an error in the code you've inputted. It's unavoidable to experience bugs when you're composing code. A bug is another word for a problem, bugs can come in numerous structures, especially when you input incorrect syntax or when the logic of input is erroneous. Thonny's bug button is normally used to spot and examine bugs.

F-H: These icons are known as the Arrow icons; their function is to enable to you run your program one-step after the other. This can be valuable when you're debugging or attempting to locate those dreadful bugs in your code. These symbols are utilized after you press the bug symbol. As you press these arrows, you'll see a yellow highlighted bar which indicates which line or area Python is assessing at that instance:

The F arrow informs Python to make a major stride, which means moving to the following line or block of code.

The G arrow instructs Python to take a little step, which means moving into every segment of a composition.

The H arrow instructs Python to exit the debugger feature.

I: The resume icon enables you to return to play mode from the debug mode. This comes in handy in situations when you no longer intend to go line by line through the code, and need your program to complete the process of running.

J: The stop icon, it enables you to put a halt to running your code. This appears to be helpful if your code runs a program that opens another window, and you need to stop that program.

Other User Interface features

To view more features that Thonny provides its users with, move to the menu bar and select the "View" dropdown. You would observe that Shell has a check mark close to it, which explains why you see the Shell area in Thonny's application window:

View	Run	Device	Tools
AST			
Assistant			
Exception			
Files			
Heap			
Help			
Object inspector			
Outline			
✓ Shell			
Stack			
Variables			
Program arguments			
Increase font size		⇧ ⌘ +	
Decrease font size		⌘ −	
Focus editor		⌥ E	
Focus shell		⌥ S	

Thonny's "View" Dropdown

Let's also go into what these options have to offer.

- Help: You'll select the Help view in case you need more information about working with Thonny. Presently this segment offers more information on the subjects such as Running Programs Step-wise, how to introduce outsider Packages, or utilizing Scientific Python Packages.

- Variables: This element can be entirely important. A variable in Python is valuable that you characterize in code. Variables include numbers, strings, or other complex data structures. This segment permits you to see the qualities doled out to the entirety of the variables in your program.

- Assistant: The Assistant is there to give you accommodating insights when you hit Exceptions or different sorts of mistakes.

Different features will get helpful as you advance your skill. You should check them once you become more conversant with Thonny!

The Code Editor

Now that you know what the User Interface is about, how about we use Thonny to compose a little program. In this segment, you'll come across the features of Thonny that will help direct you through your development work process.

- **Write Some Code**

In the code editor situated at the upper part of the UI, include these functions

def factorial(num):

```
if num == 1:

return 1

else:

return num * factorial(num - 1)

print(factorial(3))
```

• **Save Your Code**

Before proceeding, you should save your program regularly. You're instructed to implement this after pressing the play button. You can likewise do this by pressing the blue floppy disk icon or by heading off to the menu bar and choosing File > Save. Let's refer to this program as factorial.py.

factorial.py

```
1    def factorial(num):
2        if num == 1:
3            return 1
4        else:
5            return num * factorial(num - 1)
6
7    print(factorial(3))
8
```

Shell AST

```
Python 3.6.6
>>> %cd /Users/khardson/thonny-article
>>> %Run factorial.py
  6
>>>
```

•Run Your Code

So as to run your code, find and press the play icon. The result should be like this:

• Debug Your Code

To genuinely comprehend what this feature is doing, try the step feature. Take just a few large and little steps through the function to observe what's going on. Recollect you can use the arrow icons to do this.

Judging by the image, you will see that the steps will show how the PC is assessing each piece of the code. Each pop-up window resembles a little part of scratch paper that the computer is using to evaluate each section of the code. Without this wonderful element, this may have been difficult to conceptualize.

• Stop Running Your Code

Up until now, there hasn't been a need to hit the stop icon for this program, especially on the grounds that it exits when it has executed print(). Make efforts to expand the number being passed to the factorial function to 100:

```
def factorial(num):

if num == 1:

return 1

else:

return num * factorial(num - 1)
```

print(factorial(100))

At that point, step through the function. Eventually, you will notice that you will click for some time before you arrive at the end. This is an ideal time to bring in the stop button. The stop button can be beneficial to stop a program that is either purposefully or inadvertently running persistently.

Discover Syntax Errors in Your Code

Now that you have a straightforward program that works, let's break it by deliberately making a mistake in your factorial program, you'll have the option to observe how Thonny handles these kinds of issues. The purposeful error we'll be making is called a syntax error. A syntax error is a mistake that shows that your code is syntactically wrong. This implies that your code doesn't follow the appropriate way to compose Python. At the point when Python sees the blunder, it will show a syntax error to complain about your invalid code.

Let's say above the print statement, we include another print statement that says print("The factorial of 100 is:"). Now, let's include syntax errors. In the first print statement, remove the second quotation mark, and in the other, erase the second bracket. As you do this, you should observe that Thonny would highlight your Syntax Errors. Missing citations are highlighted in green, and missing brackets are highlighted in grey.

For starters, this is an essential asset that will assist you to point out any errors while you're typing. Some of the commonly normal and frustrating mistakes when you begin writing computer programs are missing quotes and mismatched brackets.

On the off chance that you have turned your Assistant View on, you will likewise see that it will give you a helpful message to direct you the correct way when you are troubleshooting. As you become more familiar with Thonny, the Assistant can be a valuable tool to assist you with getting unstuck!

The Package Manager

As you keep on learning Python, it tends to be very helpful if you want to download a Python bundle to use within your code. This permits you to utilize code that another person has composed within your program. Consider a model where you have to carry out a few estimations in your code. Rather than composing your own calculator, you can employ a third-party package called simplecalculator. You'll need Thonny's package manager to do this.

The package manager basically enables you to install packages that are useful for your program. Particularly, it enables you to include additional tools to your toolbox. Thonny has the built-in benefit of managing any situation with other Python interpreters.

To access the package manager, go to the menu bar and press Tools > Manage Packages, This should display a new window with a search field. Type simplecalculator into that field and click the Search button. After the results are displayed, go ahead and click Install to install this package. You will see a small window pop up showing the system's logs while it installs the package. As soon as this is complete, you can then utilize the simplecalculator in your code.

Your First Python Program: Hello, World!

Coming up with an easy program that displays a sentence is mostly the first thing any programmer does subsequent to setting up their coding environment. " Hello, World!" is the most prominent statement to make when writing these programs. It's just the trend, you can decide to write any sentence you like.

- Write the Program

Open your Python editor (IDLE is fine), and input these codes:

```
print("Hello World")
```

This will display the output:

RESULT

Hello World

This is presumably the most straightforward Python program you'll ever make, all things considered, it's still a Python program. Similarly as with any PC program, you can save this to a file, and include additional functionality to it later if necessary.

Inputting print("Hello World") in IDLE results in Hello World being printed to the screen.

- Save your Program

Ensure that you save your program in a file called hello.py. This is ordinarily done utilizing the editor's File > Save or similar.

At the point when you save your Python programs, use a .py file extension. The reason is that .py is the file extension that Python files use. Files saved with a .py extension can be accessed and edited with a text editor, yet they require a Python translator to run. On the off chance that you use a code editor designed for use with Python, it will identify that this is a Python document and utilize the proper syntax for highlighting, troubleshooting, etc.

- **Run your Program**

Here's the manner by which to run the program:

Open your document if you haven't opened it initially. This is commonly done via File > Open or similar. The next task is to run the file, the way in which you do this will rely upon your editor and platform.

•In IDLE, try Run > Run Module , a shortcut to this is by pressing F5.

•In Visual Studio Code, press Ctrl+Shift+B on Windows and Linux, or Command+Shift+B on Mac to run the build task (designed through your task runner).

You can likewise run the program from the terminal or command prompt. To do this, adjust the directory that the file is in (eg, cd path/to/file), at that point ,run these codes:

python3 hello.py

You can likewise utilize your editor's debugging tools to step through the program, each line in turn. It will inform you of any mistakes in your code.

- Include a Comment

Comments are a significant piece of programming. They permit you, the software programmer, to elucidate what each aspect of your code does. This is particularly significant when your program exceeds one line. Yet, it's an advisable practice to include comments as you compose the program — even while the program is little. It doesn't take much time before your program gets to a hundred (or even a huge number of) lines. In Python, comments begin with the hash character (#) that isn't a part of a string literally, and ends toward the finish of the physical line. In simple terms, if you decide to include a comment, start the line with #. Like this:

 # This is a comment

print("Hello World")

*RESULT

Hi World

As it would be very obvious, you'll notice that the comment isn't actually an output on the screen, it is faintly displayed

.

CHAPTER NINE

Turtle Snowflake

• Introduction

This project aims at creating beautiful snowflakes with Python Turtle on the Raspberry Pi. This is absolutely interesting and an efficient way to learn how to code with Python.

• How to draw with the Python Turtle

Launch the blank python template trinket and input these letters into the window that will be displayed.

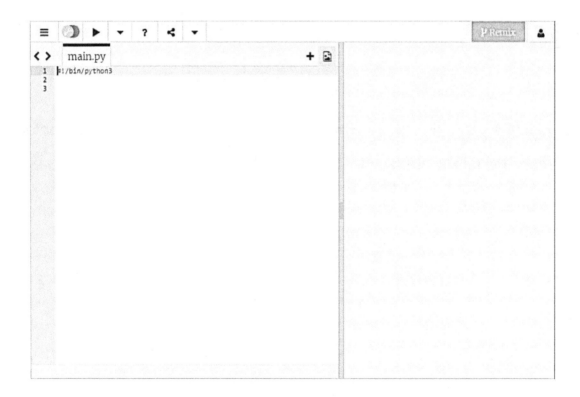

The line #!/bin/python3 just informs your computer that you're using python 3, which is the most recent version of Python. To start using Turtle in Python, you need to bring in the Turtle library. At the crest of the text editor window, input "Import Turtle." Now, give your Turtle a title, you can utilize a variable to do this. Let's call this Elsa.

- Elsa = turtle.Turtle()

Hence, you can instruct your turtle on what it should do, for instance, if you want it to forward (100)

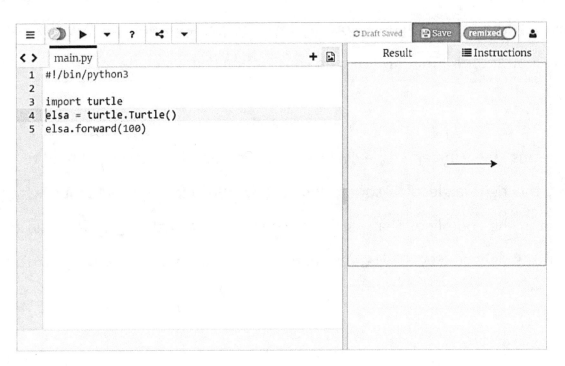

- Elsa.forward(100)

Now, click on run to test your turtle program and observes what happens

You should bear in mind that a trinket account might not be necessary if you want to save your projects. You can simply click the downward-facing arrow and then press

Link, if you don't have a trinket account. This will display a link that you can save and revert to later. However, you will need to do this each time you make any adjustments to your code, the reason being that the link will also change as you make changes to the code. And if you have already registered a trinket account, click Remix to save a duplicate of the trinket.

How to turn with the Python Turtle

You will notice that so far, your turtle has been moving in only one direction, this is satisfactory if you decide to draw straight lines. But if you intend to draw different shapes, your turtle has to turn. Now what you're going to do is, below the previous line you inputted, elsa.forward(100), in your Python code, include this:

*elsa.right(90)

Turtle terms angle in degrees, a circle has 360 degrees. Let's say we intend to build a square, the right-angle of a square would have 90 degrees, and that's why 90 is inputted in the code line. That particular code line is instructing your Turtle to turn towards the right side by 90 degrees. Input another command to move your Turtle by 100

*elsa.forward(100)

Save the code and test it and observe what happens. You will soon be creating a square. The next procedures to follow are the codes that will be included in order to complete the square.

• Using Loops to create shapes

In order to build a square, you will have to repeat some lines of code, however, this is not the most preferable way to go about this, rather than inputting several lines repeatedly, using a loop will be more efficient. This is what I'm implying:

Instead of creating a square by inputting the codes this way:

Elsa.forward(100)

Elsa.right(90)

Elsa.forward(100)

Elsa.right(90)

Elsa.forward(100)

Elsa.right(90)

Elsa.forward(100)

You can carry out this function much quicker using this:

For I in range(4):

  Elsa.forward(100)

  Elsa.right(90)

Try this, save and run the program again and notice what happens. A square will be displayed on the screen.

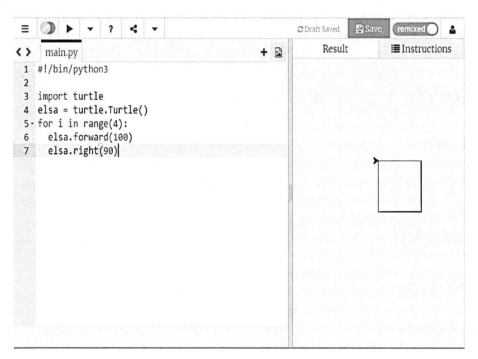

• **Creating Spiral Patterns**

Now let come to creating spirals, specifically a snowflake-like spiral. Firstly, replace the codes you inputted for your square with this:

For I in range(2):

　Elsa.forward(100)

　Elsa.right(60)

　Elsa.forward(100)

　Elsa.right(120)

Save the codes, and then run it. The outcome of this will be a parallelogram shape. You can go further to place loops inside other loops, this feature is what will help you to create a drawing that resembles a snowflake. Directly above the line for "I in range(2): " for your parallelogram codes, input this:

For I in range(10):

After inputting that, move your cursor to the line below your sequence of codes and press the spacebar four times to begin the codes you're about to write at a less distance from the margin, this is termed indenting. Indenting in Python is very essential to see to it that your code works according to your expectation. After doing that, input this:

Elsa.right(36)

Save the code and run it, and as usual, observe what happens. The outcome should be something like this:

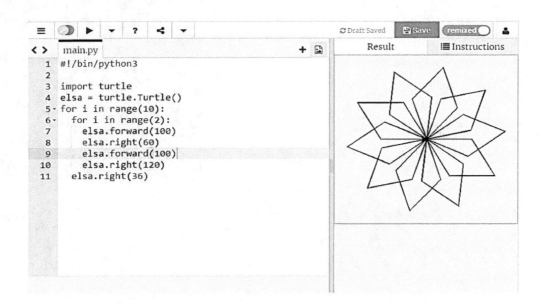

• Changing the Pen Color randomly

Until now, turtle has been drawing black lines on a white background, you should probably add some colors to it to add more aesthetics. When you want to add a color to your turtle, move your cursor below the line where you named your Turtle and before your loops, and input this:

Elsa.color("cyan")

You can use any color you like, be it red, yellow, blue, etc. You can even go further to change the color of the background window, use the instruction below the code you've just written.

Turtle.Screen().bgcolor("blue").

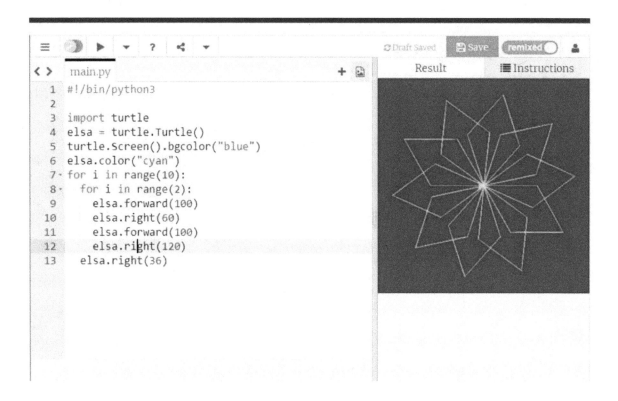

To even make it more artistic, you can include random colours for your Turtle to ensure that each time you run your code, you'll be provided with a somewhat different snowflake.

To start with, you have to import the "random" library, below the "import turtle," input "import random." The next task is to change the background color from "blue" to "grey". Just beneath that line, create a Variable called "colors" to store a list of the colors you'll choose from.

Colours = ["cyan", "purple", "white", "blue"]

At the end of the spiral loop, below elsa.right(36), input this:

Elsa.color(random.choice(colours))

Also, ensure that you indent this line so that your program stays aware that it's within the loop. Go ahead and save the codes, then run it and see a multicolored snowflake!

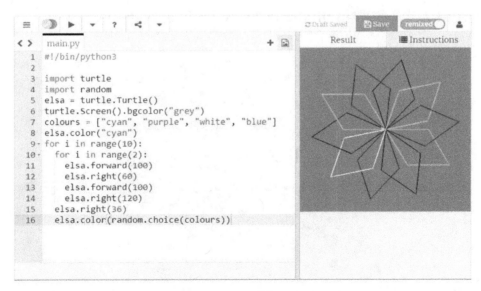

• Using a Function to draw a Snowflake

The parallelogram method of drawing a snowflake is cool,no doubt. However, the outcome clouds and it therefore doesn't exactly look like a snowflake. Using a Function to draw the snowflake will give us the perfect and exact result we're hoping.

For this drawing, we have to move the turtle from the window. The penup() and pendown() instructions enable us to do this without drawing a line, it's similar to picking a pen on a paper and taking it somewhere else on the paper to start writing. Input these instructions below the "colors" list

Elsa.penup()

Elsa.forward(90)

Elsa.left(45)

Elsa.pendown()

Then, input the code to draw a branch of the snowflake and save it in a function. Then you just simply repeat the steps multiple times to complete a snowflake.

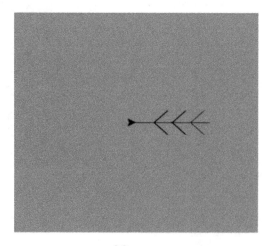

Then, define a function called "branch" by inputting this:

Def branch():

Erase the codes for the parallelogram snowflake loop and include these codes indented inside the "branch" function:

For I in range(3):

    For I in range(3):

        Elsa.forward(30)

        Elsa.backward(30)

        Elsa.right(45)

    Elsa.left(90)

    Elsa.backward(30)

    Elsa.left(45)

Elsa.right(90)

Elsa.forward(90)

Now, write a final section of code to call or run the branch function eight times, you can also employ a loop, just like you did earlier.

For I in range(8):

Branch()

Elsa.left(45)

Include a # at the start of the **"elsa.color(random.choice(colours))** instruction to change it into a comment. This implies that the computer will ignore that particular line of code. If you like, you can delete that line, however, it might be useful in case you want to include colours to your snowflake at a later time. As usual, save the code, and run it, a snowflake should appear on your screen.

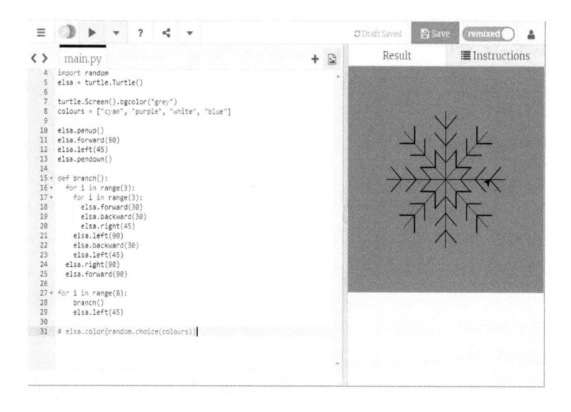

CHAPTER TEN

Physical Computing with the Raspberry Pi

Physical computing with Python: Introduction to GPIO header

Here, you will learn how to use GPIO pins on your Raspberry Pi to connect with electronic gadgets such as Light Emitting Diodes (LEDs) and Passive InfraRed Sensors (PIRS). One amazing element of the Raspberry Pi is the line of GPIO pins along the top edge of the board. GPIO represents General-Purpose Input/Output. These pins serve as links between the Raspberry Pi and the outside world. At the least difficult level, you can consider them switches that you can activate or deactivate (input) or that the Pi can turn on or off (output). The GPIO pins permit the Raspberry Pi to control and monitor the external world by being associated with electronic circuits. The Pi can control LEDs, turning them on or off, run motors, and numerous other things. It can also detect when a switch is pressed, the temperature, and light. We allude to this as physical registering. There are 40 pins on the Raspberry Pi (26 pins on early designs), and they offer several functions.

On the off chance that you possess a RasPiO pin label, it can assist with recognizing what each pin is utilized for. Ensure your pin mark is set with the keyring opening facing the USB ports, pointed outwards.

You'll see pins marked as 3V3, 5V, GND and GP2, GP3, and so forth:

3V3 (3.3 volts) - This indicates that anything associated with these pins will consistently get 3.3V of power.

5V (5 volts) - implies that anything connected with these pins will consistently get 5V of intensity of power

GND (ground) - Zero volts used to complete a circuit

GP2 (GPIO pin 2) - These pins are for general purposes and can be arranged as input or output pins.

ID_SC/ID_SD/DNC - These pins have special functions.

You should note that playing around with the GPIO pins is safe and pleasurable if you adhere to the instructions. Haphazardly plugging wires and sources of power into your Pi, may put you at the risk of destroying it, particularly if you're utilizing the 5V pins. Awful things can likewise occur if you attempt to interface things to your Pi that consume a significant amount of power, LEDs are fine, motors are definitely not. If you're concerned about this, you should consider utilizing an extra board, for instance, the Explorer HAT, until you can sufficiently handle the GPIO directly.

• Lighting an LED

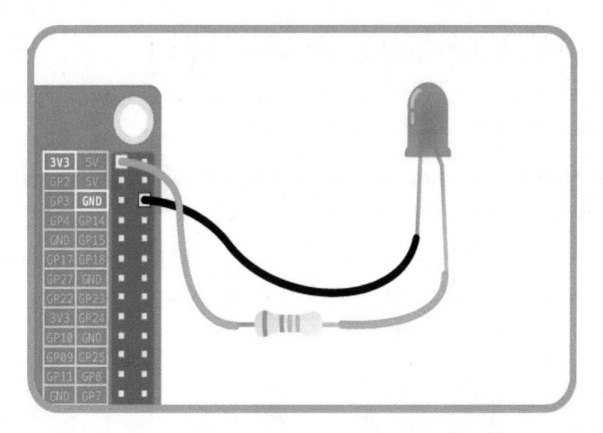

LEDs are fragile little things. If you pass a great amount of current through them, they will pop (at times tremendously). To confine the current passing through the LED, you ought to consistently utilize a resistor in series with it. Attempt to connect the long leg of a LED to the Pi's 3V3 and the short leg to a GND pin. In this type of set up, the resistor should have a value above 50 ohms. The LED should illuminate. It will consistently be on, because it's associated with a 3V3 pin, which is itself consistently on.

Let's try moving it from 3V3 to GPIO pin 17:

The LED is expected to turn off now, however it's now on a GPIO pin, and can hence be directed by code.

Switching a Light Emitting Diode on and off

GPIO Zero is another Python library which offers a much easier interface to common GPIO parts. It has been preinstalled on it by Raspbian.

Open My, then can activate or deactivate a LED by composing commands directly into the REPL. Press the REPL button in the menu bar.

Firstly, import the GPIO Zero library and instruct the Pi which GPIO pin you are working on—for a specific function, you're using pin 17.

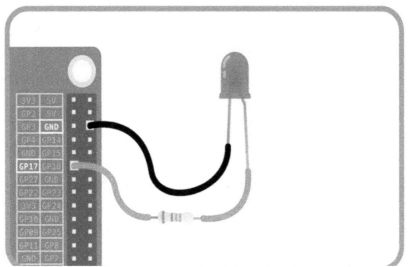

In [1]: from gpiozero import LED

In [2]: led = LED(17)

After inputting those codes, press enter on your keyboard. To enable the LED, input the following code, then press enter on your keyboard.

In [3]: led.on()

To disable the LED or switch it off, press this:

In [4]: led.off()

Flashing a Light Emitting Diode

With full assistance from "time" library, and a slight loop, you can actually cause the LED to flash. This is how you'll do it. Bring in a new file by clicking New. Then save this recent file by clicking Save. Save this file as gpio_led.py. At this point, input these codes to begin.

From gpiozero import LED

From time import sleep

Led = LED(17)

While True:

    Led.on()

    Sleep(1)

    Led.off()

    Sleep(1)

After inputting that, save the code and run it by pressing Run, this should cause the LED to keep on flashing on and off. To exit this function, press Stop.

Getting inputs with button

Up until now, you can control output components with which is a Light Emitting Diode, now let's make an attempt to connect and control input components, specifically, a button. To do this, connect the button to another GND pin and GPIO pin 2, just as it is shown in the image below:

Bring in another file by clicking "New"

- Store the file by clicking on "Save". Save the file as gpio_button.py. When you get to this stage, you'll need the " Button" class and instruct it that the button is on Pin 2, input these codes into your new file:

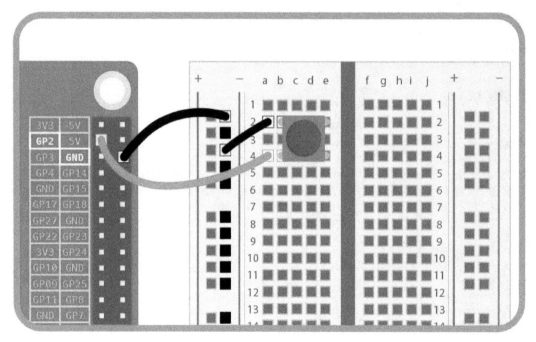

From gpiozero import Button

Button = Button(2)

Now you can get your program to carry out something when you press the button. Add these lines:

Button.wait_for_press()

Print('You pushed me')

Save and run the code.

Press the button, and your text will appear

Taking a Manual Control of the LED

Now, you can merge the two programs you've written so far to take control over the LED via the button

- Bring in a new file by pressing New. Then, save this new file by pressing " Save." Save the file in this manner, as gpio_control.py.

After doing that input these codes:

From gpiozero import LED, Button

From time import sleep

Led = LED(17)

Button = Button(2)

Button.wait_for_press()

Led.on()

Sleep(3)

Led.off(

As usual, save and run the program, the LED should be displayed for about three seconds when you when the button is pressed.

Making a Switch

When you employ a switch, pressing and releasing the button just once would switch on the LED, pressing it again would then switch it off. Adjust your codes to something like this:

From gpiozero import LED, Button

From time import sleep

Led = LED(17)

Button = Button(2)

While True:

    Button.wait_for_press()

    Led.toggle()

    Sleep(0.5)

"Led.toggle" switches the state from on to off, or vice versa. Since this occurs in a loop, the LED will turn on and off each time you press the button. It would be more preferable if you could set the LED switch on only when you hold the button down. With the aid of the GPIO Zero, that's easy. There are two categories of the Button class called " when_pressed" and " when_released." These don't block the flow of the program, so if they are entered in a loop, the program will continue to cycle unlimitedly. With that, adjust your codes to something like this:

From gpiozero import LED, Button

From signal import pause

Led = LED(17)

Button = Button(2)

Button.when_pressed = led.on

Button.when_released = led.off

Pause()

Save the program and run it, when you press the button the LED will illuminate. It will turn off again when the button is released.

Using a Buzzer

There are two basic types of a buzzer, active and passive. A passive buzzer gives out a tone when a voltage is applied across it. It also requires a specific signal to produce several tones. The active buzzers are much simpler to use, so these are covered here.

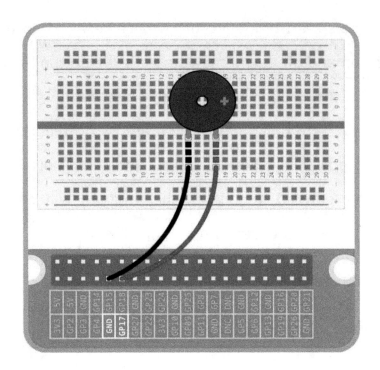

Connecting a buzzer

You can interface an active buzzer in a way that's similar to that of LED, however, due to the fact that they are a little more robust, a resistor won't be needed to protect them.

Set up the circuit as shown in the Image below;

Then, include "buzzer" to the from gpiozero import… line:

From gpiozero import Buzzer

From time import sleep

Go ahead to include a line below your creation of button and lights to add a Buzzer object:

Buzzer = Buzzer(17)

In GPIO Zero, a Buzzer works just like an LED, so try adding a buzzer.on() and buzzer.off() into your loop:

While True:

    Buzzer.on()

    Sleep(1)

    Buzzer.off()

    Sleep(1)

A Buzzer possesses a beep() method which works in a similar manner to an LED's blink. Check it out

While True:

    Buzzer.beep()

CHAPTER ELEVEN

Using a Breadboard

A Breadboard is an electronic gadget that is rectangular in shape and has numerous holes in it. The function of these tiny orifices is to allow you to insert electronic components to develop and test a version of an electronic circuit. The attachments made with the breadboard are not permanent, so perhaps you make a wrong connection, you can easily remove it and put it in the right place. The breadboard can be used to make several interesting electronic projects, be it robots, electronic drum set, electronic rain detector, and lots more.

As stated, the openings on a breadboard permit you to push the lead or metal legs of a several electronic components into them and firmly hold them into the spot. This attachment is sufficient enough such that to hold the parts to ensure they don't fall out of place, yet you can without much of a stress, snap-in or snap out a component in case you need to change/supplant it from that place. The breadboard is likewise referred to as solderless breadboards (less generally used name) – simply because you don't have to solder to bond the electronic parts together.

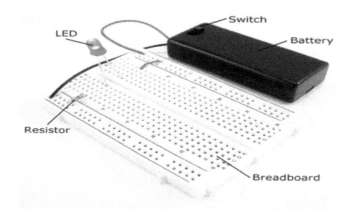

In the figure above, you see a full-sized breadboard. On either side of the breadboard, there are vertical lines or stripes normally marked with a 'red and dark' or 'red and blue' lines and also bears + or − sign. These lines are termed busses or rails and are used to convey power vertically to the whole circuit. Normally, the holes close to the red line (+) sign will associate with the positive battery terminal, and the holes close to the blue line (−) sign will interface with the negative battery terminal. The two segments within the breadboard work on a level plane. What this implies is that, on the inside, they are wired evenly, and when connected to a power source, the power streams horizontally along the line of every segment. Therefore, if you check row 1, the openings denoted as A, B, C, D, and E are connected, and the openings in lines F, G, H, I, and J are connected (this implies that power will flow from A to E and F to J).

Let's be more practical about how this works, you'll need a:

- Breadboard
- LED light
- Male-to-female jumper leads
- Male-to-male jumper leads
- 1 Resistor 10 ohms, 9-volt battery, battery snap

What we want to set up a simple LED circuit on a Breadboard

Stage 1

Take the positive (red) and the negative (dark) ends of the battery snap and place it above the power rails. After doing that, take the red wire and put one end into the gap close to the red line, at that point, take the dark wire and insert it into the gap close to the blue line.

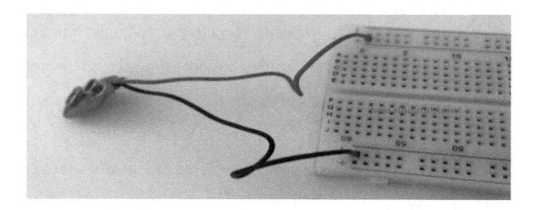

Stage 2

Next, hold the Light Emitting Diode. Take the end of the LED that is longer and put this into E15 and, after doing that, put the short end of the LED into F 45. It is pertinent that you ensure you are inserting the appropriate legs of the LED else the LED may get fused, and it will not illuminate.

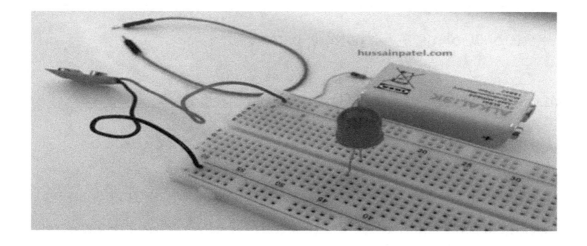

Stage 3

Here, what you have to do is to take the jumper wire and put one of its ends into opening C15, insert the other leg of the jumper wire into the power rail hole 15, located 2 openings away from E15. In fact, you can insert it in any opening on the power rail as the battery power is passing vertically through the power rail, that is from the top to the bottom.

Stage 4

Well done, you're doing perfectly fine, now, take a resistor and insert it into this into 2 openings behind F45, i.e., H45 and afterward but insert the opposite end of the resistor into the opening 45 of the power rail. In fact, you can as well insert the other end into any opening on the power rail because the battery power is passing vertically through the power rail as stated earlier.

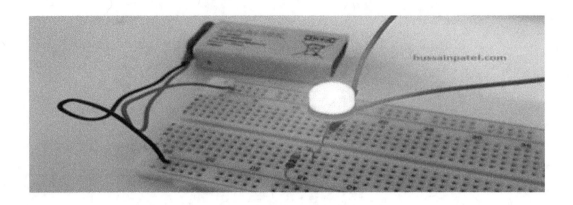

Stage 5

Inspect and Check the association again (Steps 1 to 4). After you're sure everything is in place appropriately, connect the 9-volt battery to the battery snap and the LED should glow, and there you have it!

With this demo, you've seen how to make use of a breadboard and how easy it is, provided you know the appropriate connection patterns. Also, you should have noticed how it is so natural to snap in and snap out parts.

CHAPTER TWELVE

Reading a Button on the Raspberry Pi

A good starter hardware project you can do with the Raspberry Pi is attaching a simple tactile switch to the Raspberry Pi GPIO and also detecting button functions in Python. Here, you'll gain the knowledge about how to set up a circuit with the Raspberry Pi, as well as reading the state of a button in Python. When you interface a button with Python, it grants you an entry into unlimited possibilities of actions to carry out on a button press. The items you'll need for this process include:

- A Raspberry Pi board that has been set up with the peripherals (mouse, keyboard, monitor, etc.)

- A solderless breadboard

- Jumper wire

-Resistor Pack

- A push-button, otherwise known as a tactical switch

- A multimeter, this is optional.

Setting up a Circuit

Interfacing the Raspberry Pi's multi-purpose input-output ports (GPIO) to an instantaneous push button switch is a fairly basic circuit. One side of the switch will be connected to an input pin on the Raspberry Pi, in this situation, we use Pin 10. The opposite side of the switch will be connected to the 3.3V mark on Pin 1 via a resistor.

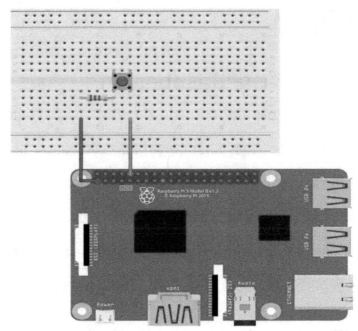

The resistor's function is to inhibit the current in order to protect the input pin by regulating the quantity of current that can flow through. The circuit is set up in this way

The notion is that the input will be relatively low because it will be at zero volts when the button is not pushed. Immediately you push the button, the pin will be instantly connected to 3.3V, and it will become relatively high because it is a 3.3V now compared to 0V. When you clamp the electronic items together to make a circuit, the reference diagram below might be of help in order to locate the correct pin numbers.

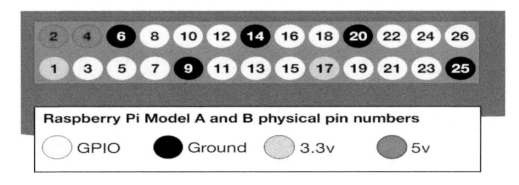

Raspberry Pi Model A and B physical pin numbers

○ GPIO   ● Ground   ○ 3.3v   ○ 5v

Composing a Python Program to read the GPIO pin

When the circuit is ready, it is necessary that we write a Python script that properly reads the status of the button and carries out the codes contingent upon the states. You must have initially installed the Raspberry Pi GPIO Python module. The Raspberry Pi GPIO Python module is a library that enables users to operate the GPIO ports directly from Python. To install the Python library, bring in a workspace, and input the following:

$ sudo apt-get install python-rpi.gpio python3-rpi.gpio

After installing this library, you can now go ahead, you can now launch your most preferred Python IDE, specifically the Thonny Python IDE, which has been treated in the earlier part of this book. The initial script will get the GPIO ports ready and then endlessly read the status of the pin until we have finished the program. With that settled, we'll now proceed to set up the library in order to utilize board numbering. We then set pin 10 as the input pin and give Raspberry Pi a directive to pull the pin low via the Pull_Up_Down features. The initialization codes are in this manner:

import RPi.GPIO as GPIO # Import Raspberry Pi GPIO library

GPIO.setwarnings(False) # Ignore warning for now

GPIO.setmode(GPIO.BOARD) # Use physical pin numbering

GPIO.setup(10, GPIO.IN, pull_up_down=GPIO.PUD_DOWN) # Set pin 10 to be an input pin and set initial value to be pulled low (off)

This pull_up_down feature in the GPIO setup informs the Raspberry Pi about the state in which the Pin is expected to be in when nothing is interfaced to it. This is vital because we want the program to read a low state anytime the button isn't pushed and a high state as soon as it is pushed. With the ports good and ready for action, we can then compose the code that analyzes the port and produces an output message when the button is pushed. The GPIO input serves to analyze the state of the port. Now, input these codes:

```
while True: # Run forever

    if GPIO.input(10) == GPIO.HIGH:

        print("Button was pushed!")
```

This program can now be executed by saving it as push_button.py and running it either in Thonny or in the console in this manner:

```
$ python3 push_button.py
```

You will observe that anytime the button is pressed, the script displays a message stating that "Button was pushed!" several times. The reason is that the state of the button is continuously being read. To resolve this issue, we can employ a GPIO event , however If after trying that option, the message still persists, or continuously outputs "Button was pushed!" without you pressing the button, try turning the button through 90 degrees.

Events based GPIO input in Python

Our goal now is to adjust our program so that it produces only a single output message anytime you press the button rather than continuously giving out the message in a spamming manner, this is where the GPIO event comes in handy. A GPIO event in the Raspberry Pi Python GPIO library functions by bringing in a Python function anytime an activity is initiated, this function is referred to as a callback function. An event can be in the form of an input being low or high, it could present itself when the pin transforms from low to high, also known as Rising, or when the pin changes from high to low, called Falling. Here, we intend to detect when a button is pressed and is at the rising edger, that is, moving from low to high.

However, before setting up the activity, we have to first write the callback function to be carried out when the event is discovered. The callback function happens to be a mundane Python function and can therefore accommodate any Python code, so it can simply print "Button was pushed!". Just above our program, we bring in the GPIO library and explain the function this way:

import RPi.GPIO as GPIO # Import Raspberry Pi GPIO library

def button_callback(channel):

   print("Button was pushed!")

After this, our programs will start up with this input pin this way:

GPIO.setwarnings(False) # Ignore warning for now

GPIO.setmode(GPIO.BOARD) # Use physical pin numbering

GPIO.setup(10, GPIO.IN, pull_up_down=GPIO.PUD_DOWN) # Set pin 10 to be an input pin and set initial value to be pulled low (off)

Now that the pin has been tagged as an input pin, we can then attach an event to it.

message = input("Press enter to quit\n\n") # Run until someone presses enter

GPIO.cleanup() # Clean up

With the codes combined, the output will resemble programs of this manner:

import RPi.GPIO as GPIO # Import Raspberry Pi GPIO library

def button_callback(channel):

   print("Button was pushed!")

GPIO.setwarnings(False) # Ignore warning for now

GPIO.setmode(GPIO.BOARD) # Use physical pin numbering

GPIO.setup(10, GPIO.IN, pull_up_down=GPIO.PUD_DOWN) # Set pin 10 to be an input pin and set initial value to be pulled low (off)

GPIO.add_event_detect(10,GPIO.RISING,callback=button_callback) # Setup event on pin 10 rising edge

message = input("Press enter to quit\n\n") # Run until someone presses enter

GPIO.cleanup() # Clean

We're almost done, just hang in there. Now save the file and execute the program via Thonny or command line with this code:

```
$ python3 push_button.py
```

From this moment onwards, you will notice that the program only displays "Button was pushed!" anytime you press the button.

CHAPTER THIRTEEN

Using a Buzzer on the Raspberry Pi 4

Abuzzer is an audio signalling device that makes a buzzing or beeping sound. They're otherwise referred to as the "annunciators". The main function of a buzzer is to inform a user that a certain action has occurred. Buzzers are of two categories: active buzzer and passive buzzer. The basic difference between the two buzzers is that active buzzers are relatively more comfortable to use, they allow the users to use it independently even when a steady direct current is applied to it, and this is what we're going to take a look at. With a continuous direct current voltage, the device will buzz at a preset frequency of 2300Hz. Technically, a buzzer operates at 5V. Because the output voltage of the GPIO pins on the Raspberry Pi are 3.3V, it appears to be a little low for a 5V buzzer. Nevertheless, the buzzer also functions at 3.3V too, however, at a 3.3 voltage supply, the intensity of sound produced by the buzzer will be lower. That being said, if you own a NPN- transistor, you can operate the buzzer at 5V, and it's advisable that you use that. Let's take a look at both hardware configurations, that is, employing 5V with transistor and using 3.3V

Setting Up the hardware components

Prior to connecting the wires to the GPIO pins of your Raspberry Pi, ensure that you have properly shut down the Raspberry Pi and removed the power cable from the board.

Using a 5 volts with a NPN transistor

- Connect the 40 pin cable present on the GPIO pins of your Raspberry Pi, you should initially remove the case of the Raspberry Pi if it calls for it. Then insert the cobbler into the breadboard just as it is in the image.

- Plug one terminal of the 40- pin cable in the cobbler. Position the buzzer on the breadboard, the long leg represents the positive leg, ensure you position it near the border of the breadboard.

- Position the NPN transistor as it is in image, the current will move from the Pin on the right side (3) to the one on the left(2), the middle pin serves as the gate. Proceed to connect the transistor pin (3) to the 5 volts pin on the Raspberry Pi 4. Interface the transistor pin (2) to Pin 23, which is the yellow wire.

- Ensure the positive leg of the buzzer is positioned on the same breadboard row as the Pin 1. After doing that, connect the negative leg of the buzzer to a GPIO GND Pin (black wire)

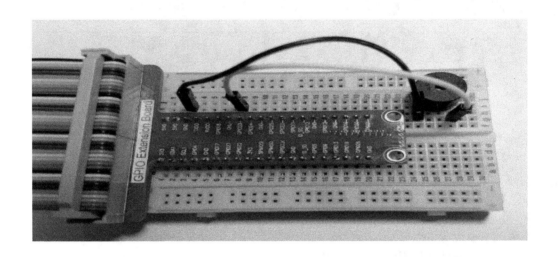

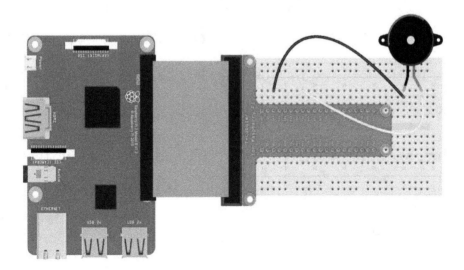

Using the 3.3V

- You should probably remove the cover of the Raspberry Pi first, and then interface the 40 pin cable on the GPIO pin of your Raspberry Pi. After that, insert the cobbler into the breadboard, as shown in the image. Plug the other terminal of the 40 pin cable in the T-cobbler.

- Position the buzzer on the breadboard such that the positive leg is placed near the border of the breadboard. Now, connect the positive leg of the buzzer to pin 23(yellow wire), and connect the negative leg of the buzzer to a GPIO GND (black wire).

Writing the code

The Thonny IDE is employed to write the codes, open the Thonny IDE on your Raspberry Pi 4 and input these codes:

```
import RPi.GPIO as GPIO

import time

GPIO.setmode(GPIO.BCM)

GPIO.setwarnings(False)

BUZZER= 23

buzzState = False

GPIO.setup(BUZZER, GPIO.OUT)
```

```
while True:

    buzzState = not buzzState

    GPIO.output(BUZZER, buzzState)

    time.sleep(1)
```

Let's go into details about every one of these codes,

GPIO.setmode(GPIO.BCM): The GPIO.BCM option implies that we are talking about the pins by the "Broadcom SOC channel" number, these are the numbers after "GPIO"

GPIO.setwarnings(False): This line of code can avoid warning messages because we don't terminate the GPIO connection properly while interrupting the program

GPIO.setup(BUZZER, GPIO.OUT): We call the BUZZER pin (=23) an output pin

while True: this serves as an infinitive loop (until we put a halt to the program)

Be careful, Python is whitespace-sensitive. Don't erase the "tab" before the next lines of code

GPIO.output(BUZZER, buzzState): This option gives each variable a value "buzzState" to the pin. Where True = 3.3V and False = 0V

time.sleep(1): hold on for 1 second

After you might have finished those processes, press the Run button. You will hear the buzzer produce a beep sound every second. To halt the beeps, press the Stop button when there's no beep sound. Well done! With this method, you can produce a sound with the buzzer on your Raspberry Pi, and you can incorporate it in an application you want to be notified by a beep sound.

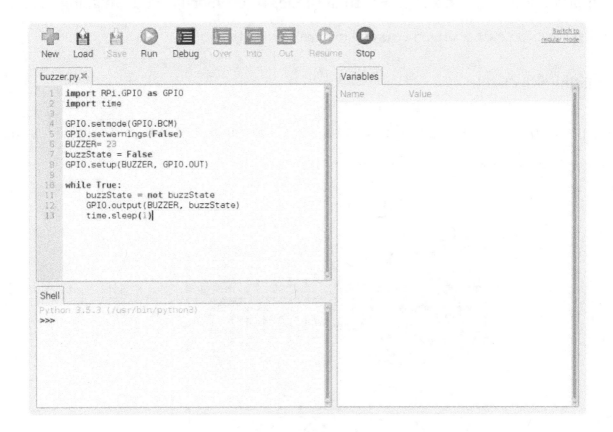

CHAPTER FOURTEEN

Python Quick Reaction Game

In this project, you will develop a quick reaction game utilizing a couple of electronic components and a Python Script. Additionally, you might need a breadboard, button, and a Light Emitting Diode. To be specific, you are going to create a quick reaction game, which you will program with Python.

● **Building the Circuit**

The circuit you will use is one that has two push-to-make buttons and an LED just as it is in the image below.

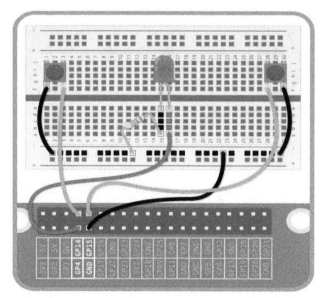

Get hold of the tactile buttons and insert it into the holes on your breadboard, with one set of legs inserted on row H and the other set inserted on row J. Do the same with the second button, placing it at the other end of the breadboard on the same row. After doing that, position an LED with the longer leg above the ridge in the breadboard in D16 and the shorter leg in D15. The numberings may vary depending on the breadboard, so ensure that you check the diagram.

That being settled, insert one leg of the resistor into column(15), this would be the short leg of the resistor, and the other leg into an opening along the blue strip. This is the point where you include the jumper wires. Begin by taking two male-to-male jumper wires and placing one end into an opening close to the outside leg of the left hand button, and the opposite end in a hole along the blue strip. Do the same for the right hand button. The next step now is to insert GPIO14 into a hole on the breadboard in line with the other leg of the left-hand button via a male-to-female jumper. Carry out this exact step for the right-hand button, but here, you will connect it to GPIO15 instead.

With the aid of another male-to-female jumper wire, insert GPIO4 to a hole on the breadboard in line with the long leg of the LED, then interface a GND GPIO pin to the blue stripe on the breadboard with the unused male-to-female jumper wire.

• **Controlling the Light**

When programming, it is advisable to deal with one problem at a time. Press the Menu>Programming>Mu. After that, click on Save As and save the file as reaction.py.

To start with, you have to bring in the modules and libraries that are essential to control the GPIO pins on the Raspberry Pi 4. Input this:

Reaction.py

Gpiozero import LED, Button

From time import sleep

While you are outputting to a Light Emitting Diode, you should create the pin through which the Light Emitting Diode connects to the Raspberry Pi in the form of output. You have to employ a variable to name the pin and then proceed to set the output.

Reaction.py

From gpiozero import LED, Button

From time import sleep

Led = LED(4)

The next thing to do is to add a couple of lines that will switch the Light Emitting Diode on, hold on for five seconds and then switch the Light Emitting Diode off.

Reaction.py

From gpiozero import LED, Button

From time import sleep

Led = LED(4)

Led.on()

Sleep(5)

Led.off()

After inputting all those, press Run to test the program.

In case the Light Emitting Diode doesn't come on for about five seconds, debug the program.

•Include an Element of Surprise

The primary aim of this game is to who presses the button immediately the light goes off, therefore the timing should be randomized. Hence, an element of surprise will be brought in, and few lines of codes need to be manipulated in order to make this happen. Directly below "from time import sleep" include a line to import uniform

From gpiozero import LED, Button

From time import sleep

From random import uniform

Led = LED(4)

Led.on()

Sleep(5)

Led.off()

In this situation, "Uniform" enables the random selection of a floating-point number (decimal) out of a range of numbers. Now, pinpoint he line "Sleep 5" and adjust it such that it reads;

From gpiozero import LED, Button

From time import sleep

From random import uniform

Led = LED(4)

Led.on()

Sleep(uniform(5, 10))

Led.off()

Then click Save so that your program is saved and click Run to confirm its effectiveness.

• Detecting the Buttons

The LED is now up and running, you might want to include a functionality in your program so that the button is detected whenever it is pressed. In that manner, you can record the scores of the players and see who emerges as the winner. As usual, you'll need to augment the codes of your current program to be able to do this.

Open the reaction.py file and input these variables below led = LED(4):

From gpiozero import LED, Button

From time import sleep

From random import uniform

Led = LED(4)

```
Right_button = Button(15)

Left_button = Button(14)

Led.on()

Sleep(uniform(5, 10))

Led.off()
```

Then, directly below "led.off()", you can insert a functionality that will be called whenever you press the button, this will inform you about the pin the button was on:

```
From gpiozero import LED, Button

From time import sleep

From random import uniform

Led = LED(4)

Right_button = Button(15)

Left_button = Button(14)

Led.on()

Sleep(uniform(5, 10))

Led.off()

Def pressed(button):
```

Print(str(button.pin.

To get over with this, when you press any of the buttons, the function will be called. If you press the "right_button," then the string can be sent to the "right" relative to the pressed function. If what you press is the "Left_button", then you're sending the string " Left."

From gpiozero import LED, Button

From time import sleep

From random import uniform

Led = LED(4)

Right_button = Button(15)

Left_button = Button(14)

Led.on()

Sleep(uniform(5, 10))

Led.off()

Def pressed(button):

Print(str(button.pin.number) + ' won the game')

Right_button.when_pressed = pressed

Left_button.when_pressed =

Now Save the program the usual way and run it.

• Get Players Name

Another cool stuff is for the program to inform you about who won rather than which button was pressed. You must first discover the players' names. You can use Input for this in Python. To discover the names of the players, you can use "input" to enter their names—below the imported libraries and modules, and the highlighted codes.

```
From gpiozero import LED, Button

From time import sleep

From random import uniform

Led = LED(4)

Right_button = Button(15)

Left_button = Button(14)

Left_name = input('left player name is ')

Right_name = input('right player name is ')

Led.on()

Sleep(uniform(5, 10))

Led.off()

Def pressed(button):
```

```
        Print(str(button.pin.number) + ' won the game')
```

Right_button.when_pressed = pressed

Left_button.when_pressed

With that, you can manipulate your pressed function, to enable it to print out the name of the winner.

From gpiozero import LED, Button

From time import sleep

From random import uniform

Led = LED(4)

Right_button = Button(15)

Left_button = Button(14)

Left_name = input('left player name is ')

Right_name = input('right player name is ')

Led.on()

Sleep(uniform(5, 10))

Led.off()

Def pressed(button):

       If button.pin.number == 14:

```
        Print(left_name + ' won the game')

    Else:

        Print(right_name + ' won the game')
```

Right_button.when_pressed = pressed

Left_button.when_pressed

- Now Save the program and run it. Debug it if it doesn't work.

Another thing you might observe is that the game doesn't quit when you push the button, this can be corrected by including an exit into the "pressed"

From gpiozero import LED, Button

From time import sleep

From random import uniform

From sys import exit

Led = LED(4)

Right_button = Button(15)

Left_button = Button(14)

Left_name = input('left player name is ')

Right_name = input('right player name is ')

Led.on()

```
Sleep(uniform(5, 10))

Led.off()

Def pressed(button):

        If button.pin.number == 14:

                Print(left_name + ' won the game')

        Else:

                Print(right_name + ' won the game')

        Exit()

Right_button.when_pressed = pressed

Left_button.when_pressed = pressed
```

In order to put the game into a loop so that the LED comes on again, remove the exit ().

Well done!

Enjoy the game!

CHAPTER FIFTEEN

Virtual Gaming with the Raspberry Pi 4

Another astonishing function of the Raspberry Pi 4 is its functionality in Virtual Reality. However, carrying out this function on the Raspberry Pi requires additional peripherals, gadgets, coding, etc. The project that will be focused on is "Be Your Hero!." This project will provide you with full gesture control of any virtual Hero you want via a couple of inexpensive devices using sensors. The entire data gathered is remotely transferred to a computer and will show your favorite hero on a normal screen or a DIY HD virtual reality headset. This project utilizes a blend of bracelets with 6-DOF sensors and Wii Nunchuck that can be joined to your body. Those sensors can identify "6 Degrees Of Freedom" with a three-axis accelerometer and a three-axis gyroscope. The central arrangement of all these embedded gadgets is an Arduino FIO fueled by a Lipo battery. The communication is enabled by an NRF24 Bluetooth board, which can balance the transmission channels. On account of this gadget, there is an enormous number of modules while interacting with a central solid Bluetooth stack.

The Bluetooth receptor is wired to an Arduino Micro. Inside this impressive board, there is an atmega32u4 (same as Arduino Leonardo) installed which enables it to imitate HID gadgets and COM ports simultaneously and on the equivalent USB line. Through this, we can duplicate a console, a mouse, a joystick simultaneously, and still send information over the serial terminal. A Raspberry Pi device can analyze the flow of data and produce the results as an interface over the HDMI. In like manner, you can as well utilize any computer operating system as the code runs on Python. The Python code enables its users with the these results:

- Full screen, which plays on the common everyday computer or TV screen

- Basic stereoscopic screen, to combine with cardboard

- Tunnel effect stereoscopic, to use on Virtual Reality headset coupled with aspheric lenses.

- Furthermore, it provides users with several methods to communicate with the "Be Your Hero" USB HID Sensor, the Keyboard, and the Mouse.

Quite a while prior, an incredible philanthropist of the Raspberry Pi community manufactured Pi3D, an extraordinary light 3D Python library running on the little CPU/GPU of our preferred PC. Here, we'll combine a Pi3D and VrZero. Also, we include a Blender which is free proficient programming to fabricate 3D objects. By searching for 3D Blender objects on the web, we'll be provided with an unlimited amount of available drawings.

HID represents " Human Interaction Devices," a USB control used for keyboards, mice and is apparently the easiest method to interact with a computer because it is recognized by virtually every operating system.

Certain Arduino boards such as Leonardo or Micro aren't utilizing the first ATmega328p AVR chip as UNO, they execute an Atmega32u4. The name doesn't appear to be totally different, nevertheless this controller will give you the chance to communicate with the USB port of a PC through HID. At moments when you are playing with an Arduino UNO, you should add a chip to interconnect the USB (like FTDI or 32u2) as HID is not compatible (aside from V-USB for AVR library, yet the execution takes more time). This HID capacity will give us an incredible method to interface among Bluetooth and Raspberry Pi since we can re-utilize a portion of the Mouse or Keyboard libraries for a straightforward interaction and furthermore utilize a Serial terminal correspondence for more intricate information moves.

The hardware gadgets you'll be making use of include:

- A Leonardo or Micro Arduino board. You can use the Micro if you intend to manage space, however you'll need an external 3.3V VCC in order to power the Bluetooth. Meanwhile, Leonardo is embedded with a 3.3V power supply which is capable of powering the Bluetooth.

- A NRF24L01+ on the SPI port

- You'll also need a button. This safety button can restrict the HID because there might be times when a wrong loop can cause your board to send multiple keyboard and mouse commands. The essential feature of a button is to carry out the command; "send nothing if button is pressed"

- Breadboard

- Load a 3D Python Map on Raspberry Pi or Any Other Platform

As you likely know, Python is now introduced on Raspberry Pi Debian, there is a major community utilizing it, and it is anything but difficult to track down some assistance. . Everything is very much reported from establishment to recording and obviously running a few demos. When you finish the installation, you can go to pi3d_demos and begin playing with all the .py you come across.

- Prepare Your Hero for Blender Custom!

Now, the 3D environment has been launched, start searching for your favorite Hero!! Blender is a verified software that can create and make adjustments to 3D objects. However, being able to use the full capacity of the tools provided is complex. Therefore, as a beginner, if you intend to create your Hero from scratch, that may be too complicated for you to do. When operating the Pi3d on a Raspberry Pi, you should be mindful of the complexity of the object, the more the vertices and complex textures, the slower the program will run.

- Enter Your Entity into Pi3d

When you see your favorite hero file, load it into Blender, the export option can then be used to create a .obj and .mtl file. However, we need to get familiar with certain things for us to successfully enter our object into pi3d : Firstly, the .obj file that will be generated entails the shape, it is vital. Also , the generated .mtl file entails the links to the colours/ texture if you import the texture of your hero from an external ".jpg" or ".png" file. Furthermore, this MTL file likewise contains the paths to locate those textures and fit them onto the appropriate surfaces. Therefore, it is very much advisable that you store the entirety of the files in a similar folder, you do this via the "copy" option when you export an object.

With that out of the way, we can now enter the entities into Pi3d by inputting this command:

Self.body = pi3d.Model(file_string="PathOfYourFile")

In case you saved the .obj, the textures and the .mtl in one folder, the Pi3d should recognize the textures and your hero should have colours. Generally, every 3D file appears to have varying sizes, our Hero is probably going to either have a large or small size. You can manipulate by inputting this:

Self.body.scale(X, X, X)

At this point, your hero should be on the map! However he's not mobile.

- Transform your 3D Hero into Multiple Objects into Several objects with Blender

Since you have imported your Hero as an entity, you can't direct your Hero's parts independently. Now, we'll revert to blender. Ideally, the goal is to separate your Hero into multiple parts. If you bring in those multiple parts into Pi3D as different objects, it will enable you to create interactions and translations between objects. However, it is pertinent that you understand certain blender functions;

Projects in Blender are termed ".blend", if you have an ".obj", you can come up with a new project and use "import .obj". The "copy" function comes in handy when you export your ".obj" so the texture is compatible with the version (paths inside ".mtl"). Include your full model, incase textures are present, choose "object mode" at the base and then press "Alt a". You will see the textures. Here are some useful keys:

-Alter the focal point by pressing the shift and the central mouse button

-The function of key A is to either select or unselect everything.

-Change the orientation of your hero on the main three axes so it's simplified : keys "r x" "r y" "r z". To make the import easier, always ensure you're at a similar reference.

- Incase you decide to rotate and centralize your hero in the center of the grid, press the three arrows.

-Press "n" and fix the 3d cursor location to 0, 0, 0.

-If you are still present in object form, you can transfer the object/transform /origin to the 3d cursor. This will enable the origin to the 3d cursor you fixed at 0,0,0.

-Proceed to save your file as blender "Full_body_hero"

At this point, let's get to splitting the hero:

Press "Save as," then term your project as "head_hero" to keep the original one. After that, choose "Edit mode" and "wire frame" at the base. You can also use Solid to visualize if there's no mistake.

When you press "C", it grants you access to the cursor. Choose all that you want to remove and press X to get rid of them. When you've removed the entire parts , press Vertex, you'll find this at the right side of where you select the mode. In a situation whereby you totally detach the neck from the head, you will discover some sort of a hole inside. Right click on the entire surrounding of the vertex of this hole and select it, then press "f" to develop a face. If the resulting face is white, it usually means that you have selected the vertex incorrectly.

With this, the first part of your hero is now available to you. You have to do the same for all the parts you want to rotate. It's a bit lengthy, but when you become more familiar with blender, it becomes faster. Do not alter the parts you are making to ensure that the cursor stays at 0.0.0. Your Hero will be well assembled when you load it into Pi3d.

• Load Your Hero in Avatar.py File

What we have to do now is to load the hero into Pi3d, this is quite easy to do, Just input this code

Self.body = pi3d.Model(file_string="PATH TO THE BODY PART .obj", name="Link");

Then insert a shader to make the texture look more attractive. Try different types and select which one suits you or your Hero , by writing this;

Shader = pi3d.Shader("uv_flat")

Input the scale to dimension your object, you'll need to do this only once. In the same manner, use the same procedure to create the head and merge the body to it with this code:

Self.body.add_child(self.head)

Now, move to run.py and replace Hero = human.link() by Hero = human.NAMEOFYOURCLASS()

When you're done, press enter and your hero will be displayed. When you've merged the entire parts, move the parts one by one. It should be responsive, however it might have wrong rotational references. You will adapt this for all objects by using cx, cy cz when you load each part. You can make several turns and manipulate the values of rotation to discover the appropriate location. Now you can load your hero, therefore run the program again, and check if it is displayed on the map.

When your hero is ready for his first mission, Be Your Hero! will permit you to initiate your first game.

Once your Hero has been fully brought in, it's high time you understood the Python code a bit more.

The code is segregated into multiple files :

Run.py is the game

Serial_data.py handles threading and serial communication

Avatar.py entails the entire links to the Hero's parts.

Map.py has all the available maps

It is not necessary that you comprehend everything to ensure it works or manipulate things. However, observe the configuration at the beginning of the game.py

```
USE_SERIAL = False
USE_STEREO = True
USE_TUNNEL = True
SHOW_STAT = True

DEFAULT_SCREEN_WIDTH=1920
DEFAULT_SCREEN_HEIGHT=1080
DEFAULT_EYE_SEPERATION=0.65

DEFAULT_AVATAR_EYE_HEIGHT = 4.0
DEFAULT_AVATAR_MOVEMENT_SPEED = 1.0
```

Here you input True or False contingent upon the configuration you want. You can insert the serial USB/HID Bluetooth, set the "USE_SERIAL" to "True" and restart your program. Change the orientation of the joystick and your nodes on, your hero will then follow you as you change position.

It's similar to enabling the entire effect : set "USE_STEREO" to True and your screen will be divided into two. "USE_TUNNEL" will enable the tunnel effect.

Conclusion

Without doubt, the Raspberry Pi 4 (and Raspberry Pis generally) is a versatile and useful device. You certainly have known more about the Raspberry Pi and its uses, it is worth every penny, it provides you with an avenue where you can play games, create software programs, develop games and numerous other function you'll do on a PC, so why not get a Raspberry Pi board for yourself and enjoy these amazing features!

ABOUT AUTHOR

Colin Schmitt is a renowned radio personality and a Programmer who has dedicated over 15 years of his life doing ham radio as a hobby. Robert enjoys teaching people and is always happy giving people all that he knows about amateur radio and coding in python programming language. Robert has participated in many emergency operations as hams where he got to display his exceptional radio skills and also write codes on the side when he is not on radio.

Robert lives in Minnesota, United States. He is happily married with two beautiful daughters.